NECROMANCY IN THE MEDICI LIBRARY

An Edition and Translation of Excerpts from
Biblioteca Medicea Laurenziana, MS Plut. 89 sup. 38

BRIAN JOHNSON

ISBN 978-1-907881-98-5 (Hardcover)
ISBN 978-1-907881-99-2 (Paperback)

A catalogue for this title is available from the British Library.

10 9 8 7 6 5 4 3 2 1

Hardcover edition printed by Biddles, Norfolk.
First published in 2020
Hadean Press
West Yorkshire
England

www.hadeanpress.com

ACKNOWLEDGMENTS

No journey – whether mythic katabasis or archival investigation – should be undertaken alone. I have enjoyed the aid of a handful of boon companions on the present intellectual adventure, whom it would be remiss of me not to recognize.

Many thanks to Dr. Alexander Cummins, for offering readers his own illuminating observations and insights upon the text in a foreword to this volume.

My manuscript transcription and translation were significantly improved at key points thanks to Daniel Harms and his knowledge of obscure lexicological matters and useful reference materials.

S. Aldarnay, with whom I have previously collaborated, once more evinced a keen artistic eye and steady hand in reproducing the manuscript's magic circles in a form infinitely superior in aesthetics to the scribe's own.

Other long-time co-conspirators are, of course, Erzebet Barthold and everyone behind the scenes at Hadean Press, who have coordinated the alchemical transmutation of my many and disparate drafts and revisions into a fully realized book.

Finally, as a matter of historical interest, I would note that the research and translation work for this book were largely conducted under conditions of mass social disruption, travel restrictions, and institutional closures during the early months of the SARS-CoV-2 pandemic, and would not have been possible had the Biblioteca Medicea Laurenziana not exhibited such admirable foresight in their manuscript digitization efforts. *Molte grazie.*

CONTENTS

The present handsome tome you bear before you is a collection of magical operations selected from a late-fifteenth-century Italian miscellany of such sorceries. Brian furnishes us with some astute textual genealogy and grimoiric context for this source material, concisely analysing its consanguinity with influential texts as diverse as the Munich Manual (MS Clm 849), the *Hygromanteia*, the *Picatrix*, the *Livre des Esperitz*, the *Pseudomonarchia daemonum*, and even a few English books of cunning. I will not bore you by repeating or attempting to summarise this good work. This foreword instead thus serves to open proceedings with a simple question: how necromantic are these rites?

The word necromancy can mean many a tenebrous thing, but we may usefully consider this collection truly necromantic in at least three strict senses, and even perhaps two further poetic senses. It contains a *necyomantic* experiment that requires a corpse. Or at least, if not the whole body, the right foot of a corpse. It includes *sciomantic* operations, concerning conjuring the shades of deceased souls to teach you any and all sciences and arts. By medieval standards, this little book of secrets certainly details various *nigromantic* sorceries trafficking with unclean spirits, spirits called "hot", and straight-up demons. Each of these types of workings – the neycomantic, sciomantic, and nigromantic – offer facets and components both familiar and novel, and as such deserve a little further survey below.

Additionally, and certainly most broadly, this collection also has a *deathly* rite that specifies fatal consequences for the nigromancer if their operation is improperly performed. Finally, as Brian affirms, I believe it fruitful to meditate on how resurrecting these unliving experiments from dusty shelves and archived catacombs to living eyes and repertoires can perform an act of textual necromancy of its very own.

But let's talk corpses for a second first. Then ghosts. Then demons. *Then* health and safety. And then the necromancing of necromancy itself.

Corpse Magic

This collection includes an operation utilising a corpse to transfer the virtues of a dead body to an object; in this case, "an unused pin". Here we may of course note a traditional distinction between *necyomancy* (deriving from the Ancient Greek root νέκυς, *nékus*, "corpse" i.e. magic employing the physical remains of the dead) and *sciomancy* (divination by the soul or shade of a deceased person) to find this collection to contain material properly necromantic by at least the first definition so far. Distinct from hauntings by the soul of the slain, or even weaponising the stain of death a violent killing leaves in a place – *the ghost of the act*, one might say – this working rather deals more directly in the potencies of a carcass itself.

This particular spell details a pin that may be employed to prevent a woman "being known by a man". Here I quite agree with the editor's assertion of this referring to "knowledge" in the colloquially Biblical sense. We have context for such sorcerous technologies, and indeed a description of a decidedly similar working from (in)famously regarded occult authorities. No less a figure than Agrippa himself details a very similar impotency operation which bears many of the features of the operation in this collection:

> Also it is said, that if a woman take a needle, and beray it with dung, and then wrap it up in earth, in which the carkass of a man was buryed, and shall carry it about her in a cloth which was used at the funerall, that no man shall be able to ly with her as long as she hath it about her.
> —Heinrich Cornelius Agrippa, *Three Books of Occult Philosophy*, trans 'J.F.' (London, 1651), 93.

These uses establish a highly relevant context for the deployment of the occult virtues of a corpse, and the effects of corpse-adjacent *materia* imbued with such virtues. The icy frigidity of death may freeze the life from the heat of passion and violence. Male sexual potency was especially framed as a hot and wet sanguine affair, further gravely decomposed by cold and dry *melancholia*.

This familiar humoural context is actually extended in this experiment to consider broader effects of the deathly pin: it can prevent people eating. Digestion – frequently referred to in pre-modern sciences of the body as *concoction* – was also envisioned in terms of a furnace heat stoking the heart's fire and vivacious warmth from our spark of life. As the pin bearing the contagious refrigerative occult virtues of a corpse's foot is placed under the foot of the living operator, death robs the living of more appetites than the strictly rapine or erotically libidinous.

Wraiths of Instruction

Most explicitly, the experiment attributed to Michael Scot contained in this anthology centres around summoning a dead tutelary shade to "benevolently, faithfully, and peacefully teach [one] all the knowledge" that one wishes. Here arguably we find a divinatory core of necromancy: raising ghosts to impart knowledge and reveal secrets.

The protocols for summoning such a tutelary spirit to appear (firstly, in order to deliver its name) require dream incubation using a talismanic cloth bundle. Significantly, the cloth is marked with the name of the spirit after it has appeared and delivered it. The talisman is thus only "completed" *by* working with the spirit, rather than before calling it. This mode of working with a spirit is not a linear matter of preparation leading to a singular potent manifestation at climax. It is an ongoing affair of multiple modalities of interaction and effect. Spirit contact and communion weaves in and out of preparations, conjurations, actions, and follow-up. Methods of dream incubation and conjuration therefore also become means of confirmation and, in this case, actually enable further steps in actions of empowerment. The blade is sharpened by use.

This back-and-forth interplay is even en-mattered in a literal dove's blood "ink" of the dreaming bundle. The circle of the pact-talisman's seal is drawn with the still-bloody heart of the sacrifice. The dove's blood is offered – performing a myriad of complex functions – and, in the course of making the offering, the working's chief talismanic tool is developed and attuned to its purpose, and becomes marked with the evidence of the sacrifice itself, as well as imbued with the various virtues of the blood of doves.

The nigromantic ritual technology evidenced in this text confirms a simple truth: these forms of conjuration are not simple one-night stands. In this case, the construction and consecration of a dreaming bundle is merely the first step of the larger work with the tutelary spirit. As has been remarked by many magicians before myself: grimoires typically actually only teach how to first call, how to prepare the circle or lamen or shewstone; or, in this case, the haunted pillow. Successful completion of conjuration instructions initiates and empowers and deepens the work. It does not necessarily "complete" it. In this case, it births the aforementioned haunted pillow. This dreaming bundle can be considered the evidence, pact, and phylactery of the relationship forged between the conjured and conjuror. It is both the materialisation of the work and the main tool manipulated to call and dispatch the spirit, by merely opening it up and folding it away, respectively.

The pact-talisman emerges from an ongoing process of call and response, consultation and action, and strategising and deepening of working relationships. The working styles and patterns described *rely on* as well as empower effective spirit contact. Without the spirit, one cannot progress in the ongoing work: not simply because the individual conjuration attempts fail, but because the next piece of the work – the next steps in the dance between practitioner and spirit in the practice – remain unknown, unheeded and unheeding, slumbering on beneath the surfaces.

And Demons

Thirdly, broaching the larger *nigromantic* contexts adumbrating the elision and interplay of devils and the dead, this collection includes a lot of demons. Explicitly identified as such, these "hot" demonic spirits are directed to visit overwhelming passions of love, hatred, and madness upon one's targets.

These spells offer a wealth of both familiar and novel names and spirits for researchers to further connect up practices and texts, enriching contexts and contrasts in practices and approaches. Variation in roles, titles, offices and relationships across various spirit-lists' shared *dramatis personae* can demonstrate dynamic and personalised engagements with these spirits and their protocols. Rich mutations can be a sign of these nigromancies' multifarious compacts and conspiracies, and not (necessarily always) mere typos and copyist errors to be corrected. There are printers' devils in the detail-telling.

Demonological grimoirists should be particularly interested in the operations involving unclean spirits demonstrating how the goetic heraldry of a spirit's office can inform image magic. Offices of many of these spirits include a prescription of a magical image relating to their listed form. A griffin spirit can empower bird effigies. A dragon empowers a metal serpent image. A spirit appearing as a soldier patronises a soldier doll spell. Beyond these specific sorceries of image and fetish, such styles of work demonstrate how zoomorphic attributes of characteristic goetic offices can be read and articulated in the very manners, means, and *materia* of one's works with a spirit of such black tomes.

Fatal Works

To end with consideration of not only the broad effects but specific ramifications of what we might most vaguely call "death(-related) magic", we can finally consider the experiment that inaugurates the present anthology. This operation specifies it has a very real, very fatal chance of outright killing a practitioner who does not correctly observe the working's timing and protocols.

The operation in question, for obtaining a literal cloak of invisibility, involves swapping clothes with the named spirits. Although the experiment outlines what will cause this death (not burning your old clothes when you go back to the conjuring place where they were relinquished), it does not detail the exact motive or means of such deadly consequences, only ominously noting this death will occur in seven days.

Death and mortality, in not only abstract but very personal and immediate ways, are present in this collection, and personal safety – let alone honouring your word and work to its fullest – should be serious considerations for the practitioner seeking to work these experiments.

Un-cursing

The present collection of sorceries has at least one further remarkable feature worthy of examination in regards to necromancy, counteracting black magic. Many cursing works detailed in this anthology have a "reverse switch", a means to bring the *maleficia* to an end. Some even instruct how to actually restore the pre-affected state and function of the target, not only stopping further damage of the curse you are working but actually reversing the harm. These include proper rites and suffumigations to facilitate ritual de-activation and not mere disposal of curse implements. They certainly supply sources of reflection, inspiration, and further analysis – in terms of tools, techniques and *materia* alone – for counter-magic, curse removal, and hex breaking.

A Necromancy of Necromancy

The editor has transcribed nigromantic excerpts from a historical work of nigromantic selections, reflexively and considerately exploring how such echoing can itself become an act of honouring. Brian states clearly in his careful introduction to the collection his motivations in his selection process for seeking both novelty and familiarity to illuminate nigromantic working paradigms. Understanding how a specifically "new" spell may indeed work by established traditional means should be an important touchstone for practitioners of many shades of black to consider carefully as we not only dredge the archives but also question the teachings of our spirits...

This little book of secrets here is a modern selection, but I believe it can be considered to follow some very traditional patterns of coherence. Our black books testify to spirits that *inter alia* swarm and multiply, thrive and starve, plot and plunder by joy-riding their contagious paper trail across discovered folios, bootleg spirit catalogues, lost manuscripts, lushly printed limited editions, furtive pamphlets, yellow-press denouncements, dark art-books, pulp grimoires, straight-up plagiary, corrupted documents, candle-shop chapbooks, and wraithly palimpsests; never mind a whole lot of tall table talk. Reprints churn goetia. We might conceive of such churn as the fertile decomposing humus of freshly paginated leaves cast from ancient trees. This fine book you read from now may light fires burning on some very old coals.

As we exhume such treasure texts dredged from the dimness of the past, we should not be so shortsighted as to contend this mere nostalgic antiquarianism or historiographical survey however. These are the remains of the conjurations of dead sorcerers. They are the anatomised components of their bodies of work. What we choose to carry forth from them, what names spoken aloud again, what deeds and deals they and their works may inspire, should sustain and empower us in return. May this print run be a libation of ink to the dead *nicromantici* themselves, and may their blessing guide your understanding, dear reader.

It is fortunate indeed that the wisdom of the dead is an infinitely renewable resource. As a friend and fellow nigromancer is fond of saying, and I am fond of quoting, *necromancy never dies*.

Dr Alexander Cummins
New England, 2020

Introduction

On the eleventh day of Christmastide, *anno domini* 1494, just as the bells of St. Peter's Basilica were summoning canons to midday prayer, in some private corner of a humble domicile tucked away amid the damp, chilly byways of Rome, a young man – perhaps with a rudimentary clerical education himself – lifted quill from paper and appraised his labors with a workmanlike satisfaction. Not exactly the pride that might accompany an original creation, but rather an eager anticipation at the prospect of turning long-held fancies into actionable plans. Indeed, with tools such as he now had at his disposal, need ambition know any limit?

Or so it may have happened. The time and place of the work's composition are known with a degree of precision uncommon for a manuscript of any genre, let alone one providing detailed instructions for inducing the infernal powers to perform any number of undertakings that religious and judicial authorities would likely consider, at best, selfish. Whether or not our scribe ever put this newly-acquired knowledge to use, the mere survival of his magical book suggests that it did not cause him to fall afoul of the law – those magicians who did usually saw their grimoires consigned to flames, even when they themselves were not.[1] At some point during the next two or three decades, however, the manuscript did leave his possession, arriving by some unguessable route among the bibliological holdings of one of the wealthiest, most influential families in Italy, two of whose scions were crowned pope during that same period.

The present volume seeks to redeem this work of necromancy from the ashes of obscurity, and in doing so, to perform an act of necromancy *stricto sensu*, raising the shades of its authors, scribes, readers and users from out of the dust to take part in a rite of commemoration and communion, that we may come to know them, if only ever so ephemerally, through the secrets they deigned to set down for posterity. In transcribing the words they read and wrote, and elucidating the sense thereof for modern tongues, I wish to honor the memory of those magi, and hope that this book might be received in the spirit of a votive, an offering at the *dies parentales* for my intellectual forebears.

---

1 Brucker, 1963: 18-19.

"Fasciculus Rerum Geomanticarum"

The codex which now bears the catalogue designation Florence, Biblioteca Medicea Laurenziana, MS Plut. 89 sup. 38, comprises a miscellany of texts, copied onto its paper leaves during the late fifteenth and potentially early sixteenth centuries, treating upon a wide variety of occult sciences. It includes approximately thirty-one distinct tracts, only one of which, falling near the middle of the codex, appears to make any explicit mention of geomancy – the title *Fasciculus rerum Geomanticarum* inscribed on its spine was evidently the work of a conscientious but ill-informed librarian at an early stage in the book's archival history. Indeed, much to the contrary, a preponderance of the materials found within deal with the ritual invocation, conjuration, and subjugation of beings variously identified as spirits or demons, alongside, and sometimes in conjunction with, the magic of astral influences or sympathetic maleficia. The contents are written in what appear to be at least four distinct hands, or possibly somewhat fewer if a scribe for some reason chose to adopt a dramatically different script for a few of the entries. The texts are mostly Latin, though the frequently unconventional orthography betrays the distinct influence of vernacular Italian – a comparison of certain texts with corresponding copies in other manuscripts discloses the extent to which a scribe might render an exemplar into a more familiar idiom. A small minority of the materials appear to be composed in a more purely vernacular dialect.

The shelfmark "Pluteus" indicates that the *Fasciculus* was part of the Medici collection prior to the establishment of the Laurentian Library; when the institution was officially opened to the public in 1571, this codex would have been resting, like some three thousand others, upon one of the library's desks (*plutei*), awaiting a curious reader. Many of those manuscripts had been collected by Cosimo the Elder, Lorenzo, and other Medici heirs before the family's expulsion from Florence in November of 1494 following Piero's disastrous negotiations with the invading force of Charles VIII of France. Other volumes were acquired by the soon-to-be Pope Leo X, Giovanni de'Medici. It was Cardinal Giovanni who shuffled the family library off to Rome for safekeeping in 1508 after reclaiming it from the Dominican convent of San Marco; the friars had purchased the Medici holdings from the city's ruling Signoria, into whose hands the books had fallen when the family was forced out of the city. As a son of Lorenzo de'Medici, Giovanni's early education took place within the orbit of no less than Marsilio Ficino and Pico della Mirandola, and he had traveled throughout western Europe in the years immediately following the Medici flight from Florence. The appreciation of humanist learning Giovanni cultivated in these formative years would lead him to further enlarge the library's catalogue during its Roman exile.

The books would finally return to Florence with the accession of another Medici, Giulio, to the papal throne as Clement VII in 1523.[2]

The only explicitly dated text within MS Plut. 89 sup. 38, falling near the end of the codex, was inscribed, according to its colophon, at Rome in January of 1494, some ten months before the Medici vacated Florence. The hand of its scribe appears to account for over one hundred of the manuscript's three hundred and twenty-five folios, with a substantial portion of these devoted to the necromantic operations which are the focus of the present volume. This individual's contributions were non-consecutive within the codex, with notable differences in ink, pen quality, and evident haste in writing, suggesting that the work was completed at various times over an extended period. The colophon of one text in this hand includes a name, Alexander, but it is not at all certain that this note was the scribe's original contribution, and not simply a trace of the exemplar being copied.

Can anything more be inferred of our copyist? Tantalizingly little: we might suppose, given the social norms and preconditions to which the study of even so anti-social a science as ritual maleficia was subject, that the codex was probably composed by a man; the significant number of operations for coercing the romantic attention of a woman certainly do not dispel this assumption. He wrote mainly in an Italian humanistic cursive script, which confirms a date in the late fifteenth to early sixteenth centuries.[3] Beyond this, and a residence in Rome if the aforementioned postscript was in fact original to this manuscript, the trail of biographical investigation goes cold. It is likewise uncertain whether the texts in markedly different scripts should be attributed to other scribes, and if so, when and where they might have been inserted relative to the dated entry. Nonetheless, it seems probable that this miscellany was acquired by the Medici during their almost thirty-year residence in Rome. The question of their role in determining any of the Codex's other contents must remain, for now, impossibly obscure.

---

2   The preceding draws upon the Biblioteca's own historical summary of their collections (https://www.bmlonline.it/en/la-biblioteca/fondi-principali/), and details of Giovanni de'Medici's biography from Concordia Seminary (https://reformation500.csl.edu/bio/pope-leo-x/). I have been unable to identify a comprehensive, modern scholarly account of Giovanni's life prior to the papacy; Vaughan's 1908 *The Medici Popes: (Leo X and Clement VII)*, while biased and outdated, is thorough in noting all of the salient points of fact.

3   Clemens & Graham, 2007: 178.

All Roads Lead to Rome

MS Plut. 89 sup. 38 is in many ways typical of late-medieval compendia of secret lore and sorcerous methods compiled for private, personal use by members of the middling educated classes. It encompasses the full spectrum of occult theory and practice popular in its day, from the geomancy of its (rather misleading) catalogue title, to alchemico-medical prescriptions, astro-magical talismans, and – the focus of this volume – rituals of black magic which explicitly call upon infernal powers. In this sense, the codex rather belies assertions of discreet typological distinctions in the collecting habits of pre-modern compilers of esoterica, and it is by no means unique in this way within its historical context.[4]

A manuscript roughly contemporary with our own, Bayerische Staatsbibliothek MS Clm 849, the so-called "Munich necromancer's handbook" (on which more anon), while it does not contain anything like the Florentine manuscript's extended theoretical treatment of the proper times at which to undertake conjurations for particular ends, its individual experiments do respect the same types of horological observations, namely the lunar phase, planetary day and hour, and, more rarely, zodiacal considerations.[5] Of course, such rubrics are practically ubiquitous in medieval manuals of conjuration, though rarely agreeing in detail. Compare, for example, the text of that prototypical grimoire, the *Magical Treatise of Solomon*, appearing in British Library MS Harley 5596,[6] a Greek manuscript also originating in a fifteenth-century Italian milieu – a particularly productive setting for inquiries of this sort, as we shall see. Even closer textual parallels can be found in Oxford, Bodleian MS Rawl. D 252, 29r-30v,[7] corroborating the advice of the Florence codex (312r) to conjure infernal spirits "when the Sun is in some warm and dry sign", and other manuscripts from equally far afield which we will address below.

At least two of the texts included in Plut. 89 sup. 38 represent titles cited by Johannes Trithemius in his 1508 bibliographic survey of proscribed magic, *Antipalus Maleficiorum*. First, beginning at 294v is the "Experimentum Michaelis Scoti nigromantici", a rather bloody operation for acquiring mundane knowledge, the incipit of which Trithemius quotes in his catalogue. This experiment is also known from the Munich manuscript. The text's colophon, attributing its composition to an Andalusian fever dream of the eponymous thirteenth-century

---

4   Cox, 2015: 10; cf. Klaassen, 2013.

5   Kieckhefer, 1998: 177.

6   Marathakis, 2011: 146 ff.

7   Klaassen, 2013: 143.

scholar, prompted at least one historian to speculate rather freely that some grain of biographical truth might be recovered from it regarding Scot's career in the circles of Frederick II's court – a prospect which, sadly, more rigorous investigations have rendered untenable.[8]

Later, on folios 313v-314r of the Florentine codex, within a concise necromantic handbook dictating the rules one must observe when undertaking to conjure, the text refers to itself as a "libro de officiis". Antedating Trithemius's mention of a "Liber officiorum" and "De officiis spirituum", if only by a little less than two decades, this is an independent early attestation of a textual tradition of demonic magic under such a name. Additional exemplars of the same genre antedating the abbot's index exist in Vatican manuscripts Barb. lat. 3589, an Occitan-Latin miscellany, and Pal. lat. 1363.[9] It is intriguing that the copyist of Barb. lat. 3589 in his *Libre de puritats*, largely derived from the *Liber Razielis*, also cites a text appearing elsewhere in the Florence codex under the incipit "Dixit Theizelius", itself a dissertation in the *Liber Razielis* tradition.[10]

A further instance of textual consanguinity occurs between the text recorded in Plut. 89 sup. 38 under the heading "In ratione cursu velocissimo..." and another fifteenth-century manuscript, bound in London Society of Antiquaries MS 39, which at 16v addresses the impossibility of conjuring demons while the canonical hours are being sung.[11] This discursus parallels a passage in the Medici codex at 313v in terms so nearly identical that the possibility of a common source text is beyond question. Moreover, both texts then proceed to follow the same basic framework in stipulating the hours of the day and night in which the various ranks of demonic nobility may be summoned, though the Florence text addresses different – or differently named – strata of the infernal hierarchy, and is rather more precise in delineating the proper hours.

And that is not the only English connection our manuscript admits: In the chapter concerning the magical uses of the psalms there is an operation for provoking a dream, which it shares with another codex in the Medici library, Plut. 89 sup. 41, 94r, as well as – along with sixteen further charms from the same collection, albeit in a somewhat mangled version – Bodleian MS Rawl. D 252, 125r-126r, also dating from the fifteenth century. Amazingly, this is still not the final text to occur in both the Oxford and Florence codicies: the latter contains a "Vinculum Salomonis" beginning on folio 116r, the same title appearing at 87v

---

8   Williams, 2003, contra Brown, 1897.

9   Giralt, 2014: 244-245.

10   ibid.: 233; see Plut. 89 sup. 38, 232r.

11   Klaassen, 1999: 158-159.

of the Rawlinson manuscript.[12] Whether or not they in fact traveled together, the diffusion of these particular texts exemplifies not only Italy's place as a key center for the copying and transmission of occult manuscripts at the close of the middle ages, but also the trans-continental nature of the networks by which those texts were circulated. As we will continue to see, Plut. 89 sup. 38 was itself an avid participant in those networks.

The Medici codex's "Experiment of Michael Scot, Necromancer" juxtaposes the magic of dream incubation with the invocation of demonic intermediaries with the dead, a methodological synthesis featuring prominently in a subset of ritual operations also found among English manuscripts of magic.[13] These sixteenth- and seventeenth-century experiments call upon a spirit by the name of Azazel or Assasel to procure the shade of a dead man, who will then impart to the magician in a dream the location of a treasure, or otherwise satisfy any curiosity the operator may have.[14] The version of this procedure recorded by Humphrey Gilbert and John Davis in February of 1567, now in British Library MS add. 36674, part of a much elaborated rite, dispenses with the incubatory element, but asks Assasel for "one of the best spirits of a dead man that ever was in the world to teach you all manner of arts appertaining to learning and hidden knowledge",[15] echoing in its pedagogical framing the Scot experiment's demand for "a certain dead spirit bearing the doctrine of all sciences, who shall benevolently, faithfully, and peacefully teach me all the knowledge that I will wish". Around a half century later, the London cunning man Arthur Gauntlet included in his personal grimoire (British Library MS Sloane 3851) an operation "To have the Spirit of a dead body" by the agency of "Asariel Aerell or Asaciell the King of the dead Or the keeper of the bones of the dead", culminating in the request that the conjured shade "bring the Book of Magical science and art",[16] recalling the Scot experiment's appeal for spiritually-imparted learning no less than Gilbert and Davis's pursuit of such tomes in their explorations of visionary necromancy.

From the magical use of the dead to the occult properties of the heavens, the Italian peninsula was a hub for the northward exchange of esoteric knowledge from around the Mediterranean as much as it was for the commerce in goods from beyond Istanbul. The royal physician John Argentine, for instance, was the only English writer to make reference to the *Picatrix* until sometime after the fifteenth century, and his knowledge of that book likely derived from a sojourn

---

12 Klaassen, 2006: 129; 2013: 137.

13 For an overview of necromantic practices in early modern England, see Harms, 2019.

14 Cummins & Legard, 2020.

15 Ibid.: 73.

16 Rankine, 2011: 235-236.

on the Continent as a medical student at Padua.[17] It should be no great surprise, then, that we discover the names of the twenty-eight lunar mansions listed in our Florentine codex to unmistakably derive from the *Picatrix* in its Latin version.[18]

Again and again, the surviving evidence seems to intimate that the Italian quattrocento saw a burgeoning in the production and reproduction of magical texts in general, and of those reflecting demonological interests in particular. It is entertaining to conjecture that the same social and economic factors that made the Italian Renaissance possible, with a vibrant economy fueling demand for the production of luxury goods of all kinds[19], also facilitated the production of illicit manuscripts, and their collection by *nouveau riche* necromancers – or at least by scholars whose patrons didn't ask too many questions. And of course, even in the worst of times, a Medici cardinal was surely able buy whatever he liked.

The apparent flurry of occult literary activity in the north of Italy during the fifteenth century, to say nothing of an elite intellectual milieu like that which propelled the publication of Marsilio Ficino's translation of the Hermetic corpus in 1471, should not, however, be permitted to create the false impression that pursuits of this kind enjoyed an atmosphere of widespread public permissiveness. As a survey of cases from the judicial records of the Florentine communal courts will attest, the practice of sorcery in the late fourteenth and early fifteenth centuries, while indeed pervasive, was by no means exempt from the attentions of both secular law and inquisitorial curia.[20] One particular case, that of Niccolò Consigli, illustrates both the career of a professional sorcerer and exorcist whose practice – at least as it is recorded in the testimony of his clients and the bill of charges against him – bore some striking similarities to certain operations detailed in the Medici codex, as well as the fate to which that profession led him. His "... invocations of demons, incantations, conjurations, adorations, immolations, and consultations for the purpose of creating infirmities in human bodies, or expelling [evil spirits]; for the purpose of revealing the future and [the whereabouts] of lost articles...; for learning and revealing secret and occult [things]...", and of course for engendering either lust or revulsion between man and woman, at his clients' discretion,[21] comprise a virtual synopsis of the rites and offices preserved in books like MS Plut. 89 sup. 38 – indeed, Consigli was said to possess just such "libros seu libellos nigromanticos".[22] He was condemned to death in 1384.

---

17   Klaassen, 2013: 49.

18   See *Picatrix*, book 4, chapter 9.

19   Goldthwaite, 1987.

20   Brucker, 1963.

21   Ibid.: 14-15.

22   Ibid.: 18.

Munich and Beyond

While a preponderance of the text of those necromantic experiments shared by
MS Plut. 89 sup. 38 and MS Clm 849 is identical, there are frequent, if minor,
discrepancies. The operation ascribed to Michael Scot, for example, as recorded
in the Florentine manuscript is superficially indistinguishable from its Munich
counterpart (minus the first two or three pages which are missing from the latter
in its present state), yet there are approximately forty variations between the two,
with greater and lesser implications for the interpretation of the text. Many, but
not all, of these can be accounted for by simple scribal error and cumulative
textual corruption, but even so neither manuscript presents a text that is more
complete or more obviously corresponds to a coherent *urtext* in every instance.
Moreover, there are a minority of cases in which a variation suggests either a
different source text, or active intervention by one of the copyists.

   Even this limited divergence is somewhat surprising, given the texts' apparently
quite circumscribed distribution – the only two manuscript witnesses to the Scot
experiment (precisely those we have considered here) appear within less than a
century of one another, each independent of any larger corpus pertaining to
Michael Scot and his legendary reputation as a magician. Within that relatively
brief window, however, some version or versions of this collection of operations
evidently traveled some six hundred miles, crossing the Alps, to bring itself to
the attention of anonymous compilers of esoterica in both Rome and Germany
(where it was probably seen by Johannes Trithemius, writing at Würzburg in 1508).
There is even evidence of a linguistic nature for the direction in which that journey
initially proceeded: commenting on an experiment in the Munich manuscript for
obtaining a magical horse (23v-25r), Kieckhefer notes that the word *squassare*, "to
shake" [the horse's bridle], "...may possibly suggest that this material derives from
an Italian source. That verb passed over into modern Italian, and may be more
expected in Latin texts from Italy than in those from elsewhere."[23] All told, the
evidence suggests the participation of these texts in the circulation of magical
manuscripts throughout a network of copyists – whether practitioners or merely
curious collectors – which must have been significantly more pervasive than the
extant material as yet identified in archives can by itself attest.

   Further adumbrations of a textual genealogy emerge from the litanies of
demonic names that are ubiquitous in this genre. Of the more than three-dozen
spirits subjected to taxonomic description in the catalogue beginning on 303r of
the Florence codex, perhaps eleven have some cognate form in the fifteenth- or

---

23   Kieckhefer, 1998: 56-57.

sixteenth-century *Livre des esperitz*, and as many as twenty-one in Johann Weyer's 1563 *Pseudomonarchia daemonum*.[24] Save for Volach and Gomeris/Caym (albeit going by the name Gaeneron), the short list beginning at 65v in the Munich manual is entirely different, though it evinces the same remarkable conformity as the others in the formulaic composition of its entries. These bare numbers, however, while apparently indicative of a fair degree of identity – and by no means insignificant – do obscure a great deal of confusion: even where names appear to agree, the rank, offices, number of subordinates, and appearance of any given spirit are all prone to omission, revision, or augmentation from one text to another, to say nothing of those cases where onomastic mutation is so severe that the remaining similarities of those very attributes provide the only hint that two entries in fact refer to the same individual. In addition, the neat hierarchy of triumvirate and quadrumvirate laid out in the *Livre des esperitz* finds no parallel in the Munich or Florence manuscript (beyond a few incoherent allusions to a king of the north in the latter), and the kings of the quarters named by Weyer are entirely different. Outside of the catalogues proper, the names of those demons invoked in the experiments shared by MS Clm 849 and MS Plut. 89 sup. 38 also evince varying degrees of orthographic juggling.

The piecemeal and unsystematic method by which most pre-modern grimoires were compiled meant that even when two such compendia drew upon textual traditions ultimately traceable to some common root, the geographically distributed, temporally extended, and essentially reflexive and organic processes by which those texts evolved ensured that each branch would bear its own unique grafts and convolutions. The origin of any given discrepancy remains obscure, but some are more puzzling than others. Variant spellings, omissions, and even differently enumerated legions might be accounted for by simple copyist's error, but substantive modifications to a spirit's appearance, or the offices they may perform, speak to some source outside of the transcription process. The unsystematic way in which these anomalies manifest across the different catalogues seems less suggestive of material interpolated from parallel textual sources, than of independent scribal innovation. We might speculate that this kind of intervention, where the creator of a manuscript crossed the boundary between amanuensis and author, was motivated by the writer's own experience of interactions with the entities delineated in the text they were studying, interactions which prompted them to "correct" that source. A novel appearance, the adoption of a new office, or even promotion or demotion in the infernal hierarchy could all derive from a copyist's active pursuit of contact with a spirit, and the responses this evoked.

---

24   These comparisons were greatly facilitated by reference to Boudet, 2003.

Indeed, the scribe of MS Plut. 89 sup. 38 obviously took more than an academic interest in the magical operations he transcribed. For instance, in one of several experiments "ad amorem", he evidently returned to his manuscript at a later date to annotate the prescription of myrrh and saffron incense, writing in the margin that the myrrh should be "Tunisian, the resin fresh", and that aloeswood could be substituted for the saffron. These are clearly reflections born of empirical observation and practical engagement with the text – "experiment" in the truest sense. (Material limitations may have played some part as well; no doubt saffron was at least as expensive in the fifteenth century as it is today!)

This Edition

The texts I have chosen to transcribe and translate for this edition represent not a cross-section or representative sample of the contents of MS Plut. 89 sup. 38, but rather a focused study upon one segment of the oeuvre of its major contributing scribe. These particular excerpts were selected in consideration of three distinct but interrelated criteria. First, they share a common paradigm of practice; even where other elements are present, all of these texts utilize the quasi-liturgical methods of conjuration and exorcism characteristic of ritual magic in late medieval Latin Christendom, conducted according to a system of propitious astrological timing. This unity allows for a coherent examination of one prominent aspect of the scribe's magical interests.

Under this broad rubric, the second and third criteria fulfill two seemingly opposed imperatives: novelty, and analogy. For the purpose of investigating heretofore unexplored textual ground, the tract bearing the incipit "In ratione cursu velocissimo...", with its unique catalogue of spirits and handbook of rules for conjuration, was an obvious choice for inclusion. Likewise, the operations titled "experimentum de speculo" and "Ut mulier non possit cognosci a, viro", while drawing their essential elements from a corpus of traditional ritual tropes, combine and redeploy these in ways both familiar and unconventional. Conversely, the remaining operations included in the present volume all have one thing in common: each appears in a substantially identical form in both MS Plut. 89 sup. 38 and MS Clm 849. This is significant not only in demonstrating the process by which groups of magical texts might have been circulated and copied together in the late medieval world, but perhaps even moreso for revealing the divergences in detail which the two manuscripts evince between their corresponding contents. From orthography, to vocabulary, to the wholesale excision (or interpolation) of entire clauses, the overwhelming textual similarity of these two manuscripts sets off their differences in stark relief, complicating any facile reconstruction of transmission history.

Notes on the Transcription and Translation

In the interest of preserving the integrity of these texts for scholarly study, while also rendering them amenable to consultation for practical purposes, I have adhered to the following editorial conventions:

Transcription

- In order to retain any orthographic features that may reflect lexical nuances peculiar to the particular social and historical milieu of the scribe, I have attempted to reproduce the spelling, capitalization, and punctuation as it appears in the original manuscript. Obvious misspellings, including transposed letters (a noticeably frequent occurrence, suggesting that the scribe was perhaps not perfectly conversant with the Latin language), have, however, generally been regularized without comment.

- Suspensions, contractions, and otherwise abbreviated forms have been expanded. This has not been indicated in the transcription or apparatus, with the exception of uncertain readings.

- Text inside <> indicates a conjectural interpretation of obscure shorthand or otherwise illegible script.

- Text in **bold** is rubricated in the original manuscript.

- Non-alphanumeric shorthand has been written out, with the first instance of each example noted in the apparatus.

- In those parts of the text which correspond to elements of Bayerische Staatsbibliothek MS Clm 849, variations have been noted only where they seem to substantively affect meaning, or provide potential codicological insight.

Translation

- Short of extensively re-structuring every passage, I have attempted to apply punctuation in a way that will convey the syntactical sense of the text to a modern reader.

- Inconsistently spelled names have been regularized according to either their most frequent form, or their first appearance in the text. The letter ẏ in proper names has been anglicized as y, or as ï where necessary to distinguish it from a diphthong.

- Text inside [] indicates an interpolation not strictly corresponding to the original text, supplied for clarification.

- Third-person speech has been placed inside quotation marks, while text intended for recitation has been italicized.

Biblioteca Medicea Laurenziana

MS Plut. 89 sup. 38

[283r]

Ad invisibilitatem:—[25]

Tracto etiam de arte invisibilitatis hodie quasi ab omnibus
ignora. Cum itaque volueris apud omnia tam ratio-
nabilia quam non invisibilis haberi. Primo cresente
luna die mercurii in prima hora diei[26] castus ante
per triduum, et tonsus capillis, et barbam: et albo indutus extra villam in loco occulto sereno caelo, in pla-
no solo, cum ense splendidissimo fac circulum, ut
hic apparet scribendo[27] cum eo omnia ibidem aparentia:
hoc facto fingas versus occidentem super firiel dictum   x
ensem, et cum figeris habeas vas in quo sit ignis cum
thure mirra, et olibano: et cum fumo ipsorum
vade circulum suffumigando ipsum incipiendo a,
firẏel, et ibi finiendo: hoc facto habeas aquam benedictam, et aspergas te et circulum dicendo. Asperge
me domine ẏsopo, et mundabor lavabis me et super
nivem dealbabor. Quo facto volvendo te genibus
flexis versus occidentem emissa voce sic dicas.
Ego .n. coniuro vos O firẏel. Melemil. Berich.
Taraor spiritus potentes magnifici, et illustres, in   xx
quibus omnino confido per unitam, inseperabilem, et
individuam trinitatem scilicet patrem, et filium, et spiritum sanctum.
Et per deum unicum solum vivum, et verum: qui omnia de nihilo formavit, et cui subdita sunt omnia caelestia,
terrestria, et infernalia: et per caelum, et terram, mare

---

25   cf. Clm 849, 28r-29v.

26   ♀ in the ms.

27   *scribendo hec nomina* in Clm 849.

For Invisibility

Likewise I have excerpted on the art of invisibility, of which, like everyone today,
you are ignorant. When, therefore, in the midst of everyone, both
rational and not, you wish to possess invisibility, first, with
the Moon waxing on the day of Mercury, in the first hour of the day, being pure
for three days beforehand, with hair and beard sheared, and
dressed in white, outside of town in a secret place under a clear sky, in
a flat place, with a sword most splendid make a circle, as
seen herein,[28] writing with it all that appears there.
This having been done, you shall set the aforesaid   x
sword toward the west, upon the name Firïel, and when you have transfixed it[29]
    take a vessel in which a fire burns with
incense of myrrh and frankincense, and with the smoke thereof
you shall perambulate the circle, suffumigating it, beginning at
Firïel and there finishing. This having been done, take
blessed water and asperge yourself and the circle, saying: *Asperge*
me, Lord, with hyssop, and I will be clean; wash me, and
I will be made whiter than snow.[30] Which being done, turn yourself, knees
bent toward the west, saying thus by the utterance of your voice:
I, [name], conjure you, O Firïel, Melemil, Berich,
Taraor, spirits powerful, magnificent, and famous, in   xx
whom I am entirely confident, by the united, inseparable, and
indivisible Trinity, namely the Father, and the Son, and the Holy Spirit.
And by the living God, singular, unique, and true, who
formed everything from nothing, and to whom are subject all the heavens,
lands, and infernal regions; and by heaven and earth, sea

---

28   Fig. 1, 284r; cf. Clm 849, 28r.

29   Reading *fixeris* for *figeris* in the ms.

30   Vulg. Ps. 50:9.

[283v]

et infernum, et omnia in ipsis existentia: et per omnes principes
reges, et dominos vestros, et per illum deum quem timetis et
adoratis: et per omnia quae habent vos terrere, constrin-
gere, et alligare: et quorum praeceptum vos opportet
totaliter adimplere, quatenus vos omnes quattuor cum humilitate maxima huc venire debeatis ligati, constric-
ti, et coniurati ad executionem mandandum quicquid
a, vobis petiero: venite sine mora, venite
quia invoco vos ex parte patris provoco vos ex parte
filii: provoco vos ex parte spiritus sancti: hec dicta quater   x
scilicet versus firẏel, semel versus Melemil, et versus
Berich semel, et Taraor semel. aderunt subito in
circulo quattuor spiritus dicentes tibi, dic nobis quid vis, et
plene tibi obediemus quibus deces. ego volo quandam
cappam invisibilitatis, quae sit tenuis et incorrup-
tibilis: qua cum indutus fuero nullus videre, nec
me sentire valeat: hoc dicto unus discedet, et
ante hora apportabit tibi quandam cappam: quam
ab ipsis interrogabas, ut tibi dare deberetur.
Qui respondebunt tibi dare non posse, si primo   xx
ipsis non das tuum indutum album: quibus dabis: et
cum dederis eis, ipsi dabunt tibi cappam quam cum[31] indue-
ris illis spiritibus dices abite cum pace et statim recedent: et cum abierint debes dimittere circulum
ferendo ensem: tercio vero die cum cappa illuc rever-

---

31   *...tibi cappam quorum unus statim induet indutum eis datum similiter tu statim induas cappam quam cum...*
     in Clm 849.

and the depths, and all which in them exists; and by all
your princes, kings, and masters; and by that God who you fear and
adore; and by all who may terrify,
bind, and hold you fast, and whose command it behooves you
to fulfill completely, insofar as all four of you with
the greatest humility must come to this place bound,
constrained, and sworn to perform whatever
assignment I shall ask of you. Come without delay, come,
for I invoke you on behalf of the Father, I call you forth on behalf
of the Son, I call you forth on behalf of the Holy Spirit. This having been said
    four times, x
namely toward Firïel, once toward Melemil, and toward
Berich once, and Taraor once,
the four spirits will suddenly arrive in the circle, saying to you, "Tell us what you
    wish, and
we will obey you fully", to which you will say: *I desire a certain*
cloak of invisibility, which is subtle and
imperishable, wearing which I shall be seen by no one, nor
shall they be able to perceive me. This having been said, one will depart and,
before an hour has passed, bring to you that cloak; which
you asked of them, so he must give it to you.
They will not be able to answer you thus, if first xx
you do not give to them your white garment; which you will give, and
when you have given it to them they will give to you the cloak, which when
you have donned, those spirits will say, "Go in peace", and at once
withdraw. And when they have gone you must quit the circle,
carrying the sword. But on the third day

[284r]

tere, et invenies tuum indutum: quem accipies. Memento
enim si ipso tercio die non reverteris sive indutum ibi di-
missum non acciperes, quarto die nihil inveni-
res, sed in septem diebus morieris. Accepto enim tercio
die induto ipsum in eodem loco comburres, et scies
quod quando ipsum combures audies maximos plantus, et
querelas: et cum combureris aspergas cinerem per aerem,
sic dicendo. Ego coniuro vos firẏel. Melemil. Berich. Taraor. Per virtutem, et potentiam vestram, et per omnia
habentia potestatem contra vos, ut non habeatis virtutem   x
nec potentiam ledendi me per hanc cappam. Sed Iesus
Christus protegat, et defendat me per omnia secula seculorum amen:—
Quo dicto habeas aquam benedictam, et aspergas dictum cappam
sic dicendo ego te coniuro cappa per patrem, et filium, et
spiritum sanctum, et per hanc aquam: ut quandocumque te indutus fuero
nullus sentire, nec videre me valeat per dominum nostrum
Iesum Christum filium dei qui vivit, et regnat per omnia secula
seculorum amen:. hic infra sunt signum speculi, et circulus penes firẏel:—

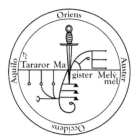

FIGURE 1

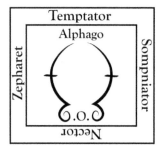

FIGURE 1B

you shall return thither with the cloak and find your garment, which you will
    claim.

For you shall remember that if on that third day you do not return, or
claim the garment there relinquished, on the fourth day
you will find nothing, but in seven days you will die. So on the third
day claim the garment, burning it up in that same place, and know
that when you burn it you will hear the greatest wailing and
lament. And when you have burned it, scatter the ash through the air,
saying thus: *I conjure you Firïel, Melemil,*
Berich, Taraor, by your virtue and power, and by all who
have power against you, so that you do not have the virtue   x
nor power to harm me through this cloak. But Jesus
Christ shall protect and defend me for all the ages of ages, amen.
Which having been said, take blessed water and asperge the aforesaid cloak,
saying thus: *I conjure you, cloak, by the Father, and the Son, and*
the Holy Spirit, and by this water, so that whenever I shall don you
no one shall be able to sense nor see me, by our Lord
Jesus Christ, son of God, who lives and reigns for all the ages
of ages, amen. Here below are the sign of the mirror,[32] and
the circle of Firïel:

---

32 See "the experiment of the mirror", 289r-290v.

Ad Amorem:—[33]

Cum volueris habere amorem a, quacumque muliere vis
sive longinqua, sive propinqua: in[34] quacumque die, ut
nocte vis: sive in augumento, sive in amicitia detri-
mento. Primo debes habere columbam totam albam, et
cartam factam de cane femina, dum est in amore.
et scias quod est potentissima ad amorem mulierum ha-
bendam, debes etiam habere calamum aquilae: et in loco
occulto accipe praedictam columbam, et eam dentibus
morde prope[35] cor, ita ut cruor[36] egrediatur: et cum ca-   x
lamo aquilae, in dicta carta cum dicto sanguine sub[37] nomen
illius quam vis habere mulieris. Fac ẏmago nudam melius
ut scis dicendo formo te talem, filiam talis quam habere
desidero nomine istorum sex spirituum calidorum scilicet Tubal.
Sathan. Reufates[38]. Cupido. Afalẏon. Duliatus[39] quod ipsa
me dilligat super omnes viventes istius mundi. Qua
facta scribe in fronte nomen ipsius, et nomen Tubal
dicendo tu es talis, filia talis de cetero ad meam
voluntatem disposita: et tu es tubal in fronte eius
te iubeo permanere ligando sensus eius capitis sui   xx
de me tantummodo cupientem: postea scribe in
brachio suo dextro Sathan, et in sinistro Reufates: quibus scriptus dic sicut tu Sathan, et Reufates estis scripti ẏmagine facta nomine talis[40] enim Ita vos
coniuro affligatis[41] brachia ista sua enim ut aliquid
facere nequeat sed me amplecti desideret:

---

33   cf. Clm 849, 8r-11v.

34   *...propinqua tam nobili quam prolipia in...* in Clm 849, Kieckhefer amending *prolipia* as *plebeia*.

35   *penes* in the ms., amended by a marginal annotation.

36   *cor* in Clm 849.

37   Inserted by annotation in the ms.; *scribe* in Clm 849.

38   *Reuces* in Clm 849 here and infra; amended as *rutes* in the ms., subsequently canceled.

39   Amended as *Duliatos* in the ms., subsequently canceled.

40   Here and infra, marginal and superscript annotations in the ms. adding *f.* [*iliam*] *t.* [*alis*] and other redundant suppletive glosses have been omitted. These emendations are not characteristic of this scribe's other contributions, and may be the work of a later reader.

41   *...ita continuo affligatis...* in Clm 849.

For Love

When you want to have the love of whatsoever woman you wish,
either far or near, in whatsoever day or
night you wish, whether affinity be increasing or
decreasing, first you must have a completely white dove, and
parchment made from a female dog while she is in heat;
and you should know that it is most potent
to have this for the love of women. You must also have the quill of an eagle.
     And in
a secret place, take the aforesaid dove, and with your teeth
bite it near the heart, such that the blood comes forth; and with   x
the quill of an eagle, in the aforesaid parchment with the aforesaid blood, under
     the name
of that woman whom you wish to have, make a nude image,
as you know the better how, saying: *I form you, so and so, daughter of so and so, whom
I desire to have, in the name of those six hot spirits, namely Tubal,
Sathan, Reufates, Cupido, Afalïon, and Duliatus, so that she
esteem me above all the creatures of this world.* Which
having been done, write on its brow her name, and the name "Tubal",
saying: *You are so and so,*[42] *daughter of so and so, henceforth
disposed to my will. And you are Tubal upon her brow;
I command you to perpetually bind the senses of her head*   xx
to desire only me. Afterwards, write on
its right arm "Sathan", and on the left
"Reufates", which having been written, say: *Just as you, Sathan and
Reufates, are written in the image made in the name of so and so, indeed so
I conjure you to afflict her arms; so that truly
she shall be unable to do anything at all except desire to embrace me.*

---

42 Nominal *talis*, i.e. the name of the individual in question.

[285r]

Quo facto iterum scribe in cor ẏmaginis nomen tuum dicendo
sicut in corde istius imaginis ita talis die noctuque me
in corde suo habeat: Quo facto scribe super vulvam
imaginis hoc nomen cupido dicendo, sicut tu cupido es super vulvam istius ẏmaginis ita semper perma-
neas super vulvam talis, accendendo ipsam: ut omnes viros istius muldi despiciat, et me tantummodo cupiat:
et ignis amoris mei ipsam torqueat, et inflammet.
Quo facto scribe in crure ipsius destro Afalẏon,
in sinistro Duliatus: quibus scriptis dic sicut tu   x
Afalẏon, et tu Duliatus estis scripti in hac ẏmagine, ita sedeatis[43]
in cruribus talis affligendo crura eius propter amorem[44] vehementem mei quod non vellit[45] ire, nec ire desideret aliquo: nisi huc. Quibus dictis accipe ipsam
ẏmaginem duabus manibus, et flexis genibus versus orientem[46] dic sic. Atra-
xi cor, et mentem talis per hanc ẏmaginem et per nomen ipsam[47]
invocatione forti, ut me diligat, cupiat, et af-
fectet: et etiam tota nocte in sompno aspiciat per
dominum nostrum Iesum Christum: qui vivet, et regnat
et imperat in aeternum. Quibus dictis habeas mirram[48]   xx
et zaffranum[49], et facto igne dictam ẏmaginem suffumiga
dicendo hanc coniurationem:—
Coniuro vos demones in hac ẏmagine scriptos per dominos
vestros quibus obedire teneamini scilicet Zobedam
Radalam, et Lorich[50] quatenus talem cuius

---

43   *sedeatis* added by marginal annotation in the ms.; present in Clm 849.

44   Forms of *amor* are occasionally represented in the ms. by an abstract trigon figure.

45   *velit* in Clm 849.

46   *versus orientem* added by superscript annotation in the ms.

47   *...et provoco in ipsam...* in Clm 849.

48   *Tunis, ceram novam* added by marginal annotation in the ms.

49   *ligni aloes* added by marginal annotation in the ms.

50   The names are rendered as *Sobedon, Badalam,* and *Lerith* in Clm 849.

Which having been done, again write on the heart of the image your name,
    saying:
Just as in the heart of this image, thus so and so
shall have me in her heart day and night. Which having been done, write upon the
    vulva
of the image this name "Cupido", saying: *Just as you,*
Cupido, are upon the vulva of that image, thus
you shall always remain upon the vulva of so and so, arousing it, so that
she shall disdain all the men of this world, and desire only me,
and the fire of love for me shall torment and inflame her.
Which having been done, write on its right leg "Afalÿon",[51]
on the left "Duliatus", which having been written, say: *Just as you,*   x
Afalïon, and you, Duliatus, are written upon this image, thus you shall sit
upon the legs of so and so, afflicting her legs with
vehement love for me, so that she shall not wish[52] nor
desire to go anywhere except hither. Which having been said, take that
image in both hands, and kneeling toward the east say thus:
I have allured the heart and mind of so and so with this image, and by
the powerful invocation of its name, that she shall esteem, desire, and
pursue me, and even behold me all night in her sleep, by
our Lord Jesus Christ, who lives, and reigns,
and rules forever. Which having been said, take myrrh   xx
and saffron, and having made a fire, suffumigate the aforesaid image,
saying this conjuration:
I conjure you demons written in this image by
your masters whom you are bound to obey, namely Zobedam,
Radalam, and Lorich, such that so and so,

---

51 Here following the form as written in the ms.

52 Reading *velit* for *vellit* in the ms., as per Clm 849.

[285v]

ẏmago est hic nomine figurata in amore meo debeatis[53]:
ut die noctuque in me cogitet, et de me speret[54],
donec cum affectu meam compleverit voluntatem:
et sicut in ista ẏmaginem scripti, et fixi estis, ita in ipsa re-
cumbatis donec de ea faciam quicquid velim. Hac
igitur coniuratione ter dicta, et facta suffumi-
gatione: habeas pila[55] cuiusdam eque, et suspen-
de dictam cartam cum dicto pilo, ita ut move-
atur ab aere: et dimitte stare illa vero die ut
sequenti, ut alio, ut quando potes ab illam mulierem   x
accedas: et procul dubio libentissime te videbit
dicens sine te stare non possum: et hoc habeas pro con-
stanti, et tuo animo faciet voluntatem, et super omnia te[56]
dilligit in aeternum si bene servaveris eius ẏmago
nomine figuratam in qua virtus talis existit: et
si esset maxima loci distantia, et velles eam aportari
a demonibus supradictis: qui[57] ita efficaces sunt quod
si esset in oriente, in una hora ipsam ab ocasu
portarent sine aliqua divulgatione: et ut sit
facta ẏmago, ut dictum est, et suspensa illa die in aliqua   xx
hora diei sufflas in ipsam: ita quod flatu tuo move-
atur, et similiter secunda die, et tercia die: In
nocte vero ipsius diei tercia, ut in prima die
solus, ut cum tribus sociis fidelibus accipe dictam ẏmaginem
et cum pilo liga ipsam ad collum tuum ut pendat in pectore

---

53   *...meo accendere debeatis...* in Clm 849.

54   Amended as *suspiret* in the ms.; *speret* in Clm 849.

55   *...habeas caude pilum...* in Clm 849.

56   *te omnia* in Clm 849.

57   Clm 849 elaborates the preceding passage: *...in qua virtus talis existit ymmo et de hoc magis est admirandum hoc est signum antequam vidisses ipsam statim facta hac ymagine cum ad eam accesseris erit de taliter filocapta quod dum te viderit quod non recedas ab ipsius coniunccione privatus ymmo de omni quod volueris contentus habebis. Si vero ad eam non possis accedere sine timore aut loci distancia aut aliquo interveniente tamen potes ipsam apportari facere per supradictos demones qui ita efficaces...*

in whose name this image is fashioned, must be in love with me,
so that day and night she shall think of me, and long for me
until she fulfills my will with affection.
And just as you are written and fixed in that image, so in her
you shall repose until I do what I wish with her. This
conjuration therefore having thrice been said, and
the suffumigation having been made, take some hair of a horse,[58] and
hang the aforesaid parchment with the aforesaid hair, so that
it thus moves in the air, and leave it thus. That very day, or
the following, or another, or when you are able,   x
you shall approach that woman, and she will be most glad to see you even
    uncertainly from afar,
saying "I cannot go on without you"; and thus you shall have her
steadfastly, and she will perform what you have a mind to desire, and
esteem you above all forever. If you well maintain the image
fashioned in her name, in which such virtue exists, and
if she is in a place most distant and you should wish her to be carried from there
by the aforesaid demons, who are so efficacious that
if she is in the east, in one hour
they shall convey her to the west without any publicity, and
the image, being fashioned as has been said, and suspended for a day,
    then in any   xx
hour of the day blow upon it, such that
it is moved by your breath, and likewise the following day, and the third.
But in the night of that third day, if not on the first day,
alone or with three trustworthy companions, take the aforesaid image,
and tie it to your neck with the hair so that it hangs upon

---

58   Reading *pilum...equi* for *pila...eque* in the ms.

[286r]

tibi: et habeas quandam ensem, et in terra fac circulum cum
dicto ense: quo facto stans intus voca sotios, qui
nihil faciant nisi quod in circulo sedeant, et ludum videant:
quos si non habueris quod melius est stillum[59] ferreum, et
circa circulum ut[60] hic apparet cum scilentio semper: quo
facto dic hanc coniurationem:—
Coniuro vos demones in hoc circulo sculptos quibus
data est potestas, vis, et potentia ducendi, et alligandi
mulieres in amorem virorum. per potentiam, et virtutem ma-
iestatis divine: et per thronos, et dominationes, et potestates   x
et principatus illius qui dixit, et facta sunt: et per illos
qui non cessant clamore una voce dicentes: Sanctus
Sanctus, Sanctus dominus deus Sabaoth, pleni sunt caeli
et terra gloria tua Oxanna in excelsis: benedictus
qui venit in nomine domini Osanna in excelsis. Et per
hec nomina pavenda, et tremenda vos scilicet Barchor
Lampoẏ. Despan, Brulor, Oronoch, maloqui.
Sacola. Gevoia. Masafin. Siartin, et Lodovil[61],
et per annulum istum qui hic est, et per innumerabiles
potentias vestras, et maiorum vestrorum quod ubicumque sitis   xx
de locis vestris sine mora surgatis, et ad talem
pergatis: et statim sine falacia, huc ipsam ducatis:
et cum voluero ipsam reportatis, et de hoc nemo
sentiat, ut perpendat: qua dicta ter versus anulum
aspiciendo audiens quandam vocem dicentem. Ecce nos

FIGURE 2.

---

59   *...est habeas stilum...* in Clm 849.

60   *...circulum scribe ut...* in Clm 849.

61   The names are rendered as *Rator, Lampoy, Despan, Brulo, Dronoth, Maloqui, Satola, Gelbid, Mascifin, Nartim,* and *Lodoni* in Clm 849.

your chest. And you shall take a certain sword, and make a circle on the ground with

the aforesaid sword; which having been done, standing within, call together your companions, who

shall do nothing except sit in the circle and watch the spectacle

(whom it is best if you do not bring). Take[62] an iron stylus, and

around the circle write as appears here,[63] remaining silent all the while. Which

having been done, say this conjuration:

I conjure you demons inscribed in this circle, to whom

are given the power, strength, and potency to lead and bind

women to love men, by the power and virtue

of the divine majesty; and by the Thrones, and Dominions, and Powers,   x

and Principalities of that one who spoke and it was done; and by those

who do not cease to utter with one voice the cry: "Holy,

Holy, Holy Lord God Sabaoth, heaven

and earth are full of your glory; hosanna in the highest; blessed

are they who come in the name of the Lord; hosanna in the highest." And by

these names fearful and terrible to you, namely

Lampoy, Despan, Brulor, Oronoch, Maloqui,

Sacola, Gevoia, Masafin, Siartin, and Lodovil;

and by that circle which is here, and by

your innumerable powers, and your superiors, that wheresoever you should be,   xx

from that place you shall rise without delay, and

proceed to so and so, and lead her here at once without deceit,

and take her back when I wish; and no one

shall perceive this or pay it close attention. Which having thrice been said,

looking across the circle you will hear[64] a certain voice saying "Behold,

---

62 Reading *habeas*, as per Clm 849.

63 Fig. 2, 286r; cf. Clm 849, 10r. The inscription "l.o.s.m.i." appears to be a contraction of "locus magistri".

64 Reading *audies* for *audiens* in the ms., as per Clm 849.

[286v]

summus, et statim eos videbis sex donzellos[65] pulchrimos:
et mittes ter eadem[66] voce dicentes. ad sumus hic
parati parere tibi benigne. Dic igitur quid vis,
et statim subito faciemus: Tu autem dices eatis ad
talem, et mihi ipsam sine mora ducatis: quibus
dictis subito recedent, et ante horam ipsam sine le-
sione portabunt: et scias quod nullus ipsorum potest in-
gredi circulum, sed ipsam aportabunt apud ipsum: et ipsa
porriget tibi manum, et intus ipsam trahis quae
aliquantulum est atonita: tamen vult libentissime   x
tecum stare. Admoneo autem te quod quanto maiorem
circulum facis melius est tibi, quia in eo potes
facere circulum, et in ipso melius extendere.
Si enim aliquid tui ultra signum circuli, malum esset
tibi venta, aut muliere omnes spiritus evaneschant:
potes enim retinere hanc mulierem in dicto circulo quantum tibi placet, quia cum mulier ingre-
ditur circulum dicere debes illis spiritibus: unus
vestrum vadat ad locum a quo talem aportavistis, et
in forma eius ibidem maneat: donec ipsam hic   xx
habuero. His dictis omnes abibunt cum silentio, cum
autem illa die, ac nocte, ac mense quando tibi placuerit ipsam ad domum volueris reverti dic sic O,
vos spiritus qui talem huc dixistis[67] accipite ipsam, et
ad domum suam portate: et quotiens voluero ipsam

---

65   *domicellos* in Clm 849; etymologically related.

66   *...et mites tibi eadem...* in Clm 849.

67   *duxistis* in Clm 849.

it is us", and at once you will see them, six young knights, fair
and mild,[68] declaring to you[69] by voice, "We are here,
prepared to benignly obey you. Say, therefore, what you wish,
and at once we will do it." And you shall say: *You shall go to
so and so, and lead her to me without delay*; which
having been said, they will suddenly withdraw, and within the hour
they will bring her without harm. And you should know that none of them can
enter the circle, except to carry her into it; and she
will extend a hand to you, and drawing her within, she
being somewhat dazed, nonetheless she will most gladly   x
remain with you. I advise you, however, that the larger
you make the circle, the better it is for you, because the larger you are able
to make the circle, the better you are able to stretch out in it.
If indeed anything of yours exceed the circular mark, evil shall
come[70] upon you, or all the spirits shall make the woman vanish.
Indeed you can keep this woman in the aforesaid
circle as long as you please, because when the woman
is brought into the circle you must say to those spirits: *One
of you shall go to the place from which you carried so and so, and
remain there in her form while*   xx
I have her here. These things having been said, all will depart in silence.
But when, whether that day, or night, or month,
it should please you to will her to return home, say thus: *O,
you spirits who led[71] so and so here, take her, and
carry her to her home; and whenever I wish,*

---

68   Reading *mites* for *mittes* in the ms., as per Clm 849.

69   Reading *tibi* for *ter* in the ms., as per Clm 849.

70   Reading *veniat* for *venta* in the ms.

71   Reading *duxistis* for *dixistis* in the ms., as per Clm 849.

[287r]

sitis in reportando subiecti. Venite igitur per
miras vestras valentias quas ineffabiliter exer-
cimini, quibus ter dictis venient quinque spiritus qui
eam te vidente portabunt: memento enim quando ipsa
egreditur circulum dicendo vale, tange eam
cum ẏmagine quam habeas ad collum, quia cum muliere moraris[72]
ad collum retinere debes ẏmaginem quia semper ipsi mulieri
invisibilis apparebis: et cum ipsa abierit dissolve
ipsam acollo tuo, et in quodam vasculo dilligenter
reconde: et ipsa recondita dilue totum circulum, et   x
secure egrediaris: et quando iterum ad te venire volue-
ris, fac ut supra. Et nota quod hoc experimentum est
efficacissimum, et in eo nullum periculum est: quo solo
experimento Salomon habebat quascumque mulieres
volebat: et de hoc dicta sufficiant pro habendis mu-
lieribus, et debet fieri cum solempnitatibus maximis
et magnis reverentiis dyarum:—

Ad amorem:— de secritis artibus ẏmaginariae:—[73]

Recipe ceram virgineam arte virginisatam, et hoc in die
Iovis[74] ut in die Solis[75] hora Veneris[76] ut hora Iovis et[77] dicta cera[78] facias ẏmaginem ad carbones sine fumo in una olla positos
et habeat magister de capillis mulieris pro qua vult

---

72 Clm 849 elaborates the preceding passage: *...ad collum qia in eternum pro hac te diliget et neminem*
    preter te videre curabit ymaginem semper interim quod cum muliere moraris...

73 cf. Clm 849, 29v-31v.

74 ♃ in the ms.

75 ☉ in the ms.

76 ♀ in the ms.

77 *ex* in Clm 849.

78 As per Clm 849; *y.* in the ms.

[287r]

you shall bring her back to me. Come, therefore, by
the wonderful strength of yours which
you ineffably exercise. Which having thrice been said, five spirits will come who
you will see carry her away. So mind you when she
exits the circle to say Farewell, touching her
with the image which you have at your neck, for when you detain the woman
you must keep the image at your neck so that
you will always appear invisible to that woman. And when she has departed,
    untie
it from your neck, and in a certain vessel carefully
hide it; and that having been hidden, erase the entire circle, and   x
nonchalantly disembark. And when
you wish her to come to you again, operate as above. And note that this
    experiment is
most efficacious, and there is no peril in it; wherefore by
this experiment alone Solomon always had whatsoever women
he wanted. And enough has been said of this for
women to be had, and it must be performed with the greatest solemnities
and divine reverences.

For Love, *or* On the Secret Arts of the Image

Take virgin wax for this virginal art,[79] and this on
a Thursday or a Sunday, in the hour of Venus or of Jupiter. From[80] the
    aforesaid wax
you shall fashion an image, to be placed in a jar with smokeless coals,
and the master shall have some hair of the woman upon whom he wishes

---

79   *arte virginisatam* is probably a pun, the implicit sense being "the art of (acquiring) a virgin".

80   Reading *ex* for *et* in the ms., as per Clm 849.

[287v]

facere: et tres filos sete rubeae, et habeas tecum cultel-
lum albi manubrii ad hoc facti: et vade ad locum
ubi artifex facit acus, et tu facias facere ab eodem
artifice in ortu[81] solis usque ad horam Saturni[82]. Deinde magister
habeat sotios[83] fideles et vadat ad arborem fructiferam,
et faciat magister circulum: et incipiat magister artem facere
sive ẏmaginem mulieris pro qua facit, semper murmuran-
do dicens tu[84] Belial, Tu Ascharoth, Tu Paẏmon ad
hoc sitis opus mihi adiutores: et similiter murmuran-
do dicens Ego formo istam ẏmaginem in amorem talis ut valeat   x
ad quod facta: et tu Belial initiale princeps ad hoc
opus sis mihi adiutor, et tunc magister faciat ẏmaginem
de praedicta cera incipiens hora Iovis descendendo usque ad
horam Saturni et sic formata ẏmagine faciat fieri magister ab artifice praedicto 9. acus qui eas faciat corpore balneatus
et nitidis vestibus indutus faciat dictas ẏmaginem[85] hora solis
usque ad horam Saturni postea magister figat[86] dictus acus
in ẏmagine ita collocando unam in capite, aliam in humero,
Dextro, tertia in sinistro, quartam ubi cor consuevit ad
hominibus assignari: dicendo sicut ista acus figitur[87]   xx
in cor istius ẏmaginis ita figatur[88] amor talis in amorem meum
quod non possit dormire, vigillare, iacere, sedere, am-
bulare quousque in meum exardescat amorem:
quinta in umbilico: sixta in femore: septima
in latere dextro: octava in sinistro: nona in anno.

---

81   *hora* in Clm 849.

82   As per Clm 849; an obscure figure in the ms., which might be interpreted as ♄ with an inverted
     hook.

83   *...habeat duos sotios...* in Clm 849.

84   *...murmurando in corde tuo tu...* in Clm 849.

85   *acus* in Clm 849.

86   *fingat* in Clm 849.

87   *fingitur* in Clm 849.

88   *fingatur* in Clm 849.

to operate, and three red bristly filaments, and you shall have with you
a small knife with a white handle made for this purpose. And go to a
place where an artisan makes pins, and you shall arrange for the same to be
    crafted by that
artisan from dawn until the hour of Saturn. Then the master
shall take trustworthy companions and go to a fruitbearing tree,
and the master shall make a circle,[89] and the master shall begin to work the art,
or rather the image of the woman upon whom he operates, always
in a murmur saying: *You, Belial; you, Ascharoth; you, Paymon,*
shall be assistants to me in this work; and likewise
in a murmur saying: *I fashion that image by the love of so and so, such that it shall be*
    efficacious   x
in bringing that about; and you, Belial, first prince,
shall be an assistant to me in this work. And then the master shall make an image
from the aforesaid wax, beginning in the hour of Jupiter, down to
the hour of Saturn. And the image having been thus fashioned, the master shall
    arrange for
the aforesaid nine pins to be made by the artisan, who shall fashion them having
    bathed his body
and donned clean, neat clothes; he shall make the aforesaid pins[90] from the hour
    of the Sun
until the hour of Saturn. Afterwards the master shall drive the aforesaid pins
into the image, arranged in this way: one in the head, another in
the right shoulder, the third in the left, the fourth where
people tend to place the heart, saying: *Just as that pin is driven*   xx
into the heart of that image, so the love of so and so shall be driven into love of me,
such that she shall be unable to sleep, wake, lie down, sit, or
walk until she blaze with love for me.
The fifth in the navel, the sixth in a thigh, the seventh
in the right flank, the eighth in the left, the ninth in the anus.

---

89   This circle is not illustrated in Plut. 89 sup. 38; cf. Clm 849, 30r.

90   Reading *acus* for *ymaginem* in the ms., as per Clm 849.

[288r]

Sic formata ẏmagine christianisses ipsam inponendo ei nomen
pro qua facis submergendo ter, et dicendo quomodo
vocatur, et respondetur nomen: et tu debes dicere
ego baptizo te .n. in nomine patris, et filii, et spiritus sancti
amen: et postea pone ẏmaginem in panno novo, et mundo di-
mittendo ab hora Solis usque ad horam Martis[91] deinde facias istam coniurationem sub arbore fructifera ad
carbones accensos, et volvat se versus[92] qua orientem
et dicet coniuro caput tuum, crines tuos, aures
tuas, gene tuae: coniuro .n. cerebrum tuum: coniuro   x
.n. tunicas cerebri tui, scilicet duram, et piam matrem[93]
coniuro oculos tuos: coniuro tunicas oculorum tuorum:
coniuro frontem tuam: coniuro os tuum: coniuro dentes
tuos: coniuro mentonem[94] tuum: coniuro nasum tuum: coniuro nares tuas: coniuro pallatum tuum: coniuro
gengivas tuas: coniuro guttur tuum: coniuro humeros tuos: coniuro spatulas tuas: coniuro pectus tuum: con-
iuro mamillas tuas: coniuro corpus tuum: coniuro um-
bilicum tuum: coniuro femur tuum: coniuro renes tuas:
coniuro latera tua: coniuro annum tuum: coniuro costas tuas: xx
coniuro vulvam tuam: coniuro genua tua: coniuro crura
tua: coniuro canodas tuas, et pedum[95] tuorum: coniuro brachia
tua: coniuro digitos manuum tuarum: coniuro epar tuum:
coniuro pulmonem tuum: coniuro bucellas tuas: coniuro
stomacum tuum: coniuro totam personam tuam: coniuro totam substantiam

---

91   ♂ in the ms.

92   ...*et volvas te versus*... in Clm 849.

93   As per Clm 849; *matoē* in the ms.

94   *mentum* in Clm 849.

95   ...*coniuro talos pedum*... in Clm 849.

The image having been fashioned thus, you shall baptize it, imposing upon it
    the name
for which you operate, submerging it thrice, and saying *What
is it named?*, and responding with the name; and you must say
I baptize you, [name], *in the name of the Father, and the Son, and the Holy Spirit,
amen.* And afterwards place the image in a new, clean cloth,
putting it away from the hour of the Sun until the hour of Mars. Then
you shall perform this conjuration under a fruiting tree,
having lit the coals, and there you shall turn yourself toward the east
and say: *I conjure your head, your hair,
your ears, your cheeks; I conjure your brain,* [name]*; I conjure*   x
the membranes of your brain, [name], *namely the dura and pia mater;
I conjure your eyes; I conjure the membranes of your eyes;
I conjure your brow; I conjure your mouth; I conjure
your teeth; I conjure your chin; I conjure your nose;
I conjure your nostrils; I conjure your palate; I conjure
your gums; I conjure your throat; I conjure
your shoulders; I conjure your shoulder blades; I conjure your chest;
I conjure your breasts; I conjure your flesh; I conjure
your navel; I conjure your thigh; I conjure your kidneys;
I conjure your flanks; I conjure your anus; I conjure your ribs;*   xx
*I conjure your womb; I conjure your knees; I conjure
your legs; I conjure the heels*[96] *of your feet; I conjure
your arms; I conjure the fingers of your hands; I conjure your liver;
I conjure your lungs; I conjure what you put in your mouth; I conjure
your stomach; I conjure your entire person; I conjure*

---

96   Reading *talos* for *...canodas tuas, et...* in the ms., as per Clm 849.

[288v]

tuam: ut non possis dormire, nec sedere, nec iacere
nec aliquid artificiale facere: donec meam libi-
dinosam compleveris voluntatem. Coniuro[97] te per deum patrem
et filium, et spiritum sanctum: per magistrum artis, per virtutem ipsius,
per Sapientiam Salomonis per verum Sabaoth. per verum Seraphẏn, per verum emanuel: per omnia corpora sanctorum quae
iacent in Roma: per Luna, et Solem, et dominum maiorem: et per lac virginis, per sanctas mariam matrem domini
nostri Iesu Christi: per eucharistiam sanctam, per corpus et san-
guinem Iesu Christi: Coniuro vos, et exorcizo vos   x
impero vobis, ut: ita sicut cervus desiderat ad fon-
tem aquarum: ita desiderat .n. ad meum amorem, et sicut
corvus desiderat cadavera mortuorum: ita desideres
tu me: et sicut cera ista liquescit a, facie ignis,
ita desideret .n. in meum amorem quod non possit[98] quiescere
usque compleverit meam voluntatem. Signa autem mulieris hec sequuntur. Solitudo involutio capitis, plo-
ratus, gemitus, percussiones, emulationes: tunc magister, sive ille qui facit: vadat ad illam, et si viderit
illam solam stantem, et sedentem: tunc corroboret magister   xx
coniurationem usque ad quintum diem, et si illa in terra
omnino consumatur: si autem fuerit in villa, aut in aliam civi-
tatem transierit, tam diu magister coniurationem faciet, quosque illa posset venire. Et in hoc fuerunt
concordes omnes nicromantici, omnes astrologi, omnes hẏspani,

---

97 As per Clm 849; *Coniure* in the ms.

98 The passage ends here with *etcetera* in Clm 849, resuming at *Signa autem...*

your whole substance, that you shall not be able to sleep, nor sit, nor lie down,
nor perform any craft until
you fulfill my passionate will. I conjure you by God the Father,
and the Son, and the Holy Spirit; by the master of arts, by his virtue;
by the wisdom of Solomon; by the true Sabaoth, by the true
Seraphim, by the true Emmanuel; by all the bodies of the saints that
lie in Rome; by the Moon and Sun and the Lord
above; and by the milk of the Virgin, by blessed Mary, mother of
our Lord Jesus Christ; by the holy Eucharist, by the body and
blood of Jesus Christ. I conjure you all, and exorcize you,   x
commanding you that just as the deer wants for
a spring of waters,[99] *so* [name] *shall want for my love, and just as*
the crow desires corpses of the dead, so
you shall desire me; and just as that wax figure is melted by fire,
so [name] *shall want for my love such that she is not able to rest*
until she fulfills my will. And the signs
which shall be exhibited by the woman here follow: solitude, pensiveness,
lamentation, sighing, violence, envy. Then
the master, or the one who operates, shall go to her, and if he should see
her standing or sitting alone, then the master shall continue with   xx
the conjuration for five days, and if she
is always in the locality, the operation may be consummated; if, however, she
    should be in a village, or
she should have traveled to another city, for so long as the master
performs the conjuration she may still come to him. And in this
are agreed all the necromancers, all the astrologers, all the Spanish,

---

99   Paraphrasing Vulg. Ps. 41:2.

[289r]

Arabici. Hebrei, Caldei. Greci, et latini. Et extractum
fuit istud experimentum de secretis artibus ẏmaginariae
artis, de floribus omnium experimentorum:—

Ad Amorem:— experimentum de speculo:—
Hanc sequentem coniurationem repete quinquies, et hoc fac
die Mercurii[100] luna crescente in crepusculo noctis, et scribe
hanc figuram in unum speculum, et hec nomina cum .O. sinis-
tri anularis, et sic obdormias eandem nocte super speculum: Sinis quod ab sit tunc franges. hec sunt nomina
Temptator, Somniator, Necthor, hec est coniuratio.
Ibades tu demon coniuro te, et contestor per illum qui te
creavit, condempnavit ut hanc virtutem in hoc
speculo infundas qua si quecumque mulier, ut virgo   x
ut vidua inspexerit statim amore meo ardeat.
Item coniuro te per patrem, et filium, et spiritum sanctum: et per incar-
nationem domini mei Iesu Christus, et per passionem eius: et per
formam humanam eius, quam propter genus humanam asum-
psit, et per captivitatem eius, et per probra, et sputa, et ir-
risiones, et accusationes colophas: et per omnia mala
quae in hoc mundo sustinuit: et per resurectionem,
et gloriosam ascensionem eius, et per spiritum quae in hunc
mundum deus in discipulos suos miscit: et per confortationem
spiritus sancti, qua discipulo Christus confortavit: ut huic   xx
speculo talem virtutem infundas, ut quecumque mu-

---

100 ☿ in the ms.; for pre-modern variations on the symbol of Mercury and other heavenly bodies,
     see Evans, 1998: 350-351.

[289r]

Arabs, Hebrews, Chaldaeans, Greeks, and Latins. And
this experiment of the secret arts
of the crafting of an image was extracted from among the best of all
    experiments.

For Love, or The Experiment of the Mirror

You shall repeat this following conjuration five times, and do this
on the day of Mercury, the Moon waxing, in the twilight of the evening,[101] and
    write
this figure in a mirror,[102] and these names
from right to left in a ring around a circle, and thus you shall sleep that same
    night upon
the mirror, lying so as not to then break it. Here are the names:
Temptator, Somniator, Necthor. Here is the conjuration:
Ibades, you demon, I conjure and call you to witness by the one who
created and condemned you, that
you shall infuse this virtue into this mirror, by which if whatsoever woman,
    whether maiden   x
or widow, shall inspect it, at once she shall burn with love for me.
Likewise I conjure you by the Father, and the Son, and the Holy Spirit; and by
the incarnation of my Lord Jesus Christ, and by his passion; and by
his human form, which for the human race
he assumed; and by his bondage, and by the abuse, and spitting, and
mockery, and the accusations and blows,[103] *and by all the evils*
that endure in this world; and by
his resurrection and glorious ascension, and by the spirit which
God mixed into his disciples in this world; and by the encouragement
of the Holy spirit, by which Christ has given courage to his disciple, that
into this   xx
mirror you shall infuse such virtue, that whatsoever

---

101 cf. 313v concerning the prescribed time for conjuring the "principal demons".

102 Fig. 1b, 284r.

103 Reading *accusationes et colaphos* for *accusationes colophas* in the ms. Alternatively, it is possible
    that the text represents a scribal error for *accusationes caiaphas*, "accusations of Caiaphas"; the
    respective interpretations seem equally plausible in context.

[289v]

lier ut virgo ut vidua inspexerit ut statim in
amore meo ardeat, sicut tres reges in amore dei
ardebant. Anesa tu demon qui seduxisti Adam, et
evam te coniuro per patrem, et filium, et spiritum sanctum, ut se-
ducas illam enim cum hoc speculum intuita fuerit, ut ita in
amore meo ardeat, sicut beata virgo in amore dei:
et coniuro te propter omnes elimosinas quae propter deum date sunt
et per omnia beneficia quae propter deum facta sunt in hoc mundo: et per omnes missas quae propter deum cantate sunt, ut dicte
sunt. Coniuro te per omnia nomina dei abscondita, et ma-　　　　　　　　x
nifesta: et per istud nomen quod scribitur quatuor litteris
scilicet AGla, et per alpha, et ω, et per istud nomen quod dicitur
tetagramaton[104]: et per istud nomen quod habuit deus ab
origine mundi: ut hanc virtutem in hoc speculo infundas: ut quecumque mulier, ut virgo, ut vidua
intuita fuerit: ut statim in meo amore ardeat,
ita qua nullam requiem sui corporis habeat: donec omnem
meam adimpleat voluntatem. Ensa tu demon
coniuro te, et contestor per patrem, et filium, et spiritum sanctum,
et per omnia nomina dei, et per vigintiquatuor seniores, et per　　　　　　　　xx
Ieiunium domini nostrum Iesus Christus: et per redemptionem domini nostrum
　　　Iesus Christus
quando humanam genus redemit. Coniuro te per resurectionem domini nostrum Iesus Christus et per ascensionem eius. Coniuro
te per adventum domini nostrum Iesus Christus in novissimo die cum erit
indicare vivos, et mortuos: ut hanc virtutem

---

104 sic.

woman, whether maiden or widow, shall inspect it, at once
shall burn with love for me, just as the three kings
burned with love fir God. Anesa, you demon who seduced Adam and
Eve, I conjure you by the Father, and the Son, and the Holy Spirit, that
you shall indeed seduce her when this mirror is inspected, so that thus
she shall burn with love for me, just like the Blessed Virgin with the love for God;
and I conjure you by all the alms which are given on account of God,
and by all the kindnesses which are done in this
world on account of God, and by all the masses which are sung or
said on account of God. I conjure you by all the hidden and   x
manifest names of God, and by that name which is written in four letters,
namely AGLA, and by alpha and omega, and by that name which is called
Tetragrammaton, and by that name which God has possessed since
the beginning of the world, that
you shall infuse this virtue into this mirror, so that whatsoever woman, whether maiden or
    widow,
when it is inspected shall at once burn with love for me,
so that her body shall have no rest until
she fulfills all my will. Ensa, you demon,
I conjure and call you to witness by the Father, and the Son, and the Holy Spirit;
and by all the names of God, and by the twenty-four elders;[105] and by   xx
the fast of our Lord Jesus Christ, and by the redemption of our Lord Jesus Christ,
for it ransomed the human race. I conjure you by the
resurrection of our Lord Jesus Christ, and by his ascension. I conjure
you by the advent of our Lord Jesus Christ in the last day when he will
judge the living and the dead, that

---

105 See Revelation 4:4.

[290r]

in hoc speculo infundas: ut quecumque mulier vel
virgo, ut vidua intuita fuerit, ut statim ut <placatus>[106] et
me super omnes viros diligat. Kaos tu demon qui diu
humanitatem confundisti, te coniuro, te contestor per patrem
et filium, et spiritum sanctum: et per tres quos Nabuchdonasir[107]
rex combure nitebatur scilicet Sẏdrach. Misach. Et Ab-
denago: et per tres reges quos herodes nitibatur mar-
tirizare: et per istud nomen messias, et per istud nomen
quod dicitur Adonaẏ: et per Lxxii. Nomina Dei, et per flagellatio-
nem domini nostrum Iesus Christus et per circumcisionem eius: et per
    reprobationem   x
cum aiudeis fuerat reprobatus: et per osculationem quam
Iudas ei intulit quando ipsum tradidit in manus Iudeorum
ut hanc virtutem ut supra:—
Ibades. Anesa. Ensa. Kaos vos demones coniuro per patrem,
et filium, et spiritum sanctum, et per beatam Mariam matrem domini nostrum
    Iesus Christus
et lac beate virginis Marie, et per ubera eiusdem virginis marie: et per omnes angellos, et archangelos Dei, et per
cherubẏn, et seraphẏn. Tronos, dominationes, principatus,
potestates, et omnes apostolos dei: et per omnes martires dei: et per
omnes confessores dei: et per omnes virgines, et viduas dei: et per   xx
evangelistas dei Matheum, Marchum, Lucam, et Ioannem:
et .24. seniores: et per omnia quae deus creavit in celo, et in
terra, et in omnibus abẏsis: et per ligationem domini nostrum Iesus Christus et
per spineam coronam domini nostrum Iesus Christus et per clavos eius, qui
    manus
et pedes suos transfixerunt: et per vulnerationem domini nostrum Iesus Christus

---

106 *p9.* in the ms.

107 sic.

you shall infuse this virtue into this mirror, so that whatsoever woman, whether

maiden or widow, when it is inspected shall at once be pleased, and

esteem me above all men. Kaos, you demon who long

confounded humanity, I conjure you, I call you to witness by the Father,

and the Son, and the Holy Spirit; and by the three who

King Nebuchadnezzar tried to burn up, namely Shadrach, Meshach, and

Abednego;[108] *and by the three kings who Herod sought*

to martyr;[109] *and by that name Messiah, and by that name*

which is called Adonai, and by the seventy-two names of God; and by the

flagellation of our Lord Jesus Christ, and by his circumcision, and by his condemnation   x

when he was condemned by the Jews, and by the kiss which

Judas gave to him when he betrayed him into the hands of the Jews,

that... "hanc virtutem" *as above.*[110]

Ibades, Anesa, Ensa, Kaos, I conjure you demons by the Father,

and the Son, and the Holy Spirit; and by blessed Mary, mother of our Lord Jesus Christ,

and the blessed milk of the Virgin Mary, and by the breasts of that same

Virgin Mary; and by all the Angels and Archangels of God, and by

the Cherubim and Seraphim, Thrones, Dominions, Principalities,

Powers, and all the apostles of God; and by all the martyrs of God, and by

all the confessors of God, and by all the virgins and widows of God; and by   xx

the Evangelists of God, Matthew, Mark, Luke, and John;

and the twenty-four elders; and by all that God created in heaven, and on

the earth, and in every abyss; and by the binding of our Lord Jesus Christ, and

by the thorny crown of our Lord Jesus Christ, and by his nails, which

transfixed his hands and feet, and by the wounding of our Lord Jesus Christ,

---

108 See Daniel 3.

109 The reference is presumably to Herod I; while there are numerous medieval traditions concerning the later career of the magi, including their martyrdom in a foreign land, the ascription of responsibility to Herod is anomalous. Cf. Harris, 1959.

110 i.e. proceed with the established formula "you shall infuse this virtue into this mirror..." etc.

[290v]

et per potationem fellis, et aceti mixti: et per omnes virtutes
caelorum, ut in hoc speculo hanc virtutem venire fa-
ciatis: et infundatis: ut quecumque mulier ut virgo,
ut vidam intuita fuerit, ut nullam requiem sui corporis habeat: neque sedendo, neque stando, neque dormi-
endo, neque vigillando, neque comedendo, neque bibendo,
neque aliquid faciendo: donec meam omnem voluntatem
impleat:—

Ad dementiam cuiusvis:—[111]

Ad hoc igitur ut scientia sive ars possit ab aliquo auferri,
unde dilligenter attendere debes enim primo decrescente Luna die sabati ad illum quem dementem venire
volueris et coram eo sic dicatur plana voce subintret
Mÿrael cerebrum tuum, et omnem scientiam, sensum, et
discretionem, cogitationem dilluat, et oboleat[112]. Coniuro
te Mÿrael per omnes principes, et maiores, et per omnia quae
facere vales[113] ut in tali quem aspicio debeas permanere donec mihi libuerit: et ipsum taliter offuscare:
ut omne quod agnoscit amittat, alioquin mittam te in
maris profundum quod non egredieris in secula. Quibus
dictis recede, et prestolare, donec sero fuerit: quo facto
vade ad hostium eius, et incide de ligno ipsius hostii tantum quod de ipso calamum facere possis, et ad domum redeas:
et fac de ipso calamum, et de sanguine murilegi in
panno lini cum ipso calamo scribe. O, Mÿrael ablator

x

---

111 cf. Clm 849, 6r-7v.

112 *aboleat* in Clm 849.

113 *voles* in Clm 849.

and by the drinking of the gall mixed with vinegar; and by all the virtues
of the heavens, that
you shall infuse and make this virtue come into this mirror, so that whatsoever woman, whether maiden
or widow, when it is inspected
her body shall have no rest, neither sitting, nor standing, nor
sleeping, nor awake, nor eating, nor drinking,
nor doing anything, until
she fulfills all my will.

To Make Someone Lose Their Senses

With this, then, one shall be able to steal both knowledge and skill from
     someone,
whence carefully attend: First of all, then,
the Moon waning, on a Saturday, go to that one whom
you wish to become mad, and in their presence speak thus in a firm voice:
Mirael shall infiltrate your brain, and all knowledge, sense,
discernment and reason he shall wash away and abolish.[114] *I conjure*
you, Mirael, by all the princes and superiors, and by all which
you are able to perform, that in so and so whom I behold you must
remain as long as it pleases me, and in such a manner render them dull,   x
so that they shall let slip away all that they discern; else I shall cast you into
the depths of the sea, from which you will not rise for ages. These things
having been said, withdraw, and wait until he is implanted, which having been
     done
you shall go to that one's door,[115] and cut from the wood of that door[116]
enough that you are able to make a stylus from it, and return home
and make of it a stylus; and with the blood of a cat, upon
a linen cloth, write with that stylus: "O, Mirael, who takes away

---

114 Reading *aboleat* for *oboleat* in the ms., as per Clm 849.

115 Reading *ostium* for *hostium* in the ms.

116 Reading *ostii* for *hostii* in the ms.

[291r]

sapientiae scientiae cognitionis, et artis adsis in sensibus
talis, et ipsum[117] facere debeas animo dementem qua convocationem
scripta sic in dicto panno circulus cum dicto sanguine
ut hic apparet: et scribatur nomen illius quem privare
volueris in medio circuli conscribatur: hoc nomen Mẏrael, quibus factis debes dicere sic. Coniuro vos x.
malignos spiritus scilicet Oreoth. Idinen[118]. Otel. Trẏboẏ. Norẏoth. Belferich. Camoẏ. Ascaroth. Sobronoẏ. Sẏs-
mael: per individuam trinitatem scilicet per patrem, et filium, et
spiritum sanctum ab utroque procedentem: et per tremendam et timen-   x
dam diem Iudicii: et per omnia quae fuerunt, et sunt, et erunt,
ut sicut in hoc circulo figurati estis circuite talem: ut
ita vere, et efficaciter et existenter personam eius circuatis:
et sensus eius taliter affligatis quod ignorans demens, stul-
tus, et mente captus efficiatur. Et tu Mẏrael de
cerebro eius numquam egrediaris manes in eo die noctuque
donec ab eo abire voluero, ut iubebo. Quibus sic ter
dictis iterum redeas in eadem nocte ad domum ipsius
cum dicto panno: et cum quodam cutello: et cum ibidem fueris
volve humeros versus suum hostium, et flectens te   xx
in terram minge, et parte eius more camelli faciendo
foveam subterando dictum pannum in eius limite: dic sic
sub terro te talem in nomine demoniorum scriptorum circa
te: ut omnis tua[119] virtus sepulta sit. Et cohoperto dicto
circulo cum terra redeas iterum ad domum, et fac candelam

---

117 *spiritum* in Clm 849.

118 *Pinen* in Clm 849.

119 ...*scriptorum circa te, quod semper ipsi demones circa te et omnis tua...* in Clm 849.

wisdom, knowledge, learning, and skill, you shall come to be present within the
    senses

of so and so, and you must make that one demented in psyche." Which
    conjuration

having been written, in the aforesaid cloth there shall be made a circle as follows
    with the aforesaid   blood

as it appears here,[120] and the name of that one whom

you have wished to deprive shall be composed in the middle of the circle, where
    the name

Mirael is. These things having been done, you must say thus: *I conjure you ten*
wicked spirits, namely Oreoth, Pinen,[121] *Otel, Tryboy,*
Norioth, Belferich, Camoy, Ascaroth, Sobronoy,
Sysmael, by the indivisible Trinity, namely by the Father, and the Son, and
the Holy Spirit proceeding from both of them; and by the terrible and   x
fearful Day of Judgment; and by all who have been, and are, and will be,
that just as in this circle you are figured, so encircle so and so, so that
you shall thus indeed effectively and actually encircle that one's person,
and so afflict their faculties that
they become ignorant, mad, foolish, and their mind taken captive. And you, Mirael,
shall never disembark from their brain, remaining there day and night
until I wish you to depart from there, as I will command. These things thus

having thrice been said, you shall again return that same night to that one's
    home

with the aforesaid cloth, and with a certain small knife, and when you are there

you shall turn your back toward their door,[122] and bending   xx

toward the ground you shall urinate in[123] their direction, in the manner of a
    camel. Making

a hole, bury the aforesaid cloth in their path, saying thus:
I bury you, so and so, in the name of the demons written around
you, so that all of your virtue shall be buried. And covering the aforesaid
circle with earth, you shall return again to your home, and make a candle

---

120 Fig. 3, 292r; cf. Clm 849, 6v.

121 Reading *Pinen* for *Idinen* in the ms., as per Clm 849 and infra.

122 Reading *ostium* for *hostium* in the ms.

123 Reading *in* for *et* in the ms.

in qua scripta sint omnia contenta in circulo, et debes
ipsam de cera primo empta nomine, destructione
eius, cum uno acu similiter empta: qua facta accende
ipsam, et dic sic. Sicut hec candela facta in destructionem
talis comburitur, et consumatur: ita omnis virtus, et
scientia existens in ipso in dementiam convertatur per virtutem demoniorum in hac candela scriptorum: ut sicut vos demones hic scripti ardetis, ita nullam
requiem habere possitis: donec hoc duxeritis ad ef-
fectum. Quibus verbis semel prolatis, dictam cande-   x
lam extingue, dicendo hec verba: sicut hec candela extinguitur, ita omnis virtus in tali perma-
nens penitus consumetur. Mane autem ipsam accende
dicendo: sicut hec candela etcetera. Item alio mane
usque ad terminum septimum dierum computato primo
die. In octavo vero die videbitis illum dementem omnino
de quo omnes mirabuntur: mirabile est autem quod non
credit se habere aliquem defectum, et omnes alios mente
captos putat esse[124]. Hanc igitur experimentiam apud
te tene, quia magne virtutis est: cum autem ipsam   xx
volueris in statum pristinum, ut priorem devenire,
optime fieri potest die Iovis[125] quinta[126] hora[127] noctis vade
ad suum hostium ubi sepelisti pannum, quod dum sepelitur
debet poni pannus in quodam vase ut not putrescat,
si facis ipsam liberari[128]: et ipsum pannum desepeliendo sic

---

124 ...*mente putat esse carentes* in Clm 849.

125 2|3. in the ms.

126 .*1.* in Clm 849; the first hour of a Thursday night would place the operation in the hour of the
      Moon, whereas the present text places it in the hour of the Sun.

127 *1.* in the ms.

128 ...*putrescat sic factis omnino ipsum liberandi* in Clm 849.

[291v]

upon which shall be written all that is contained in the circle (and you must
do this upon first acquiring the wax), in the name of, and for the destruction
of, that person, with a pin likewise acquired. Which having been done, light
it, and say thus: *Just as this candle made for the destruction*
of so and so burns up and is consumed, so all the virtue and
knowledge that exists in that one shall be turned to madness by
virtue of the demons written in this candle; so
just as you demons written here burn, thus
you shall be able to have no rest until you have drawn this to
completion. These words having once been tendered,   x
extinguish the aforesaid candle, saying these words: *Just as this*
candle is extinguished, so all the virtue
remaining within so and so will be consumed. In the morning, however, light it,
saying: *Just as this candle*, etcetera. Do likewise each morning
for seven days, reckoned from the first
day. Verily, on the eighth day you will see that one entirely mad,
at which everyone will marvel; but it is astonishing that
they do not believe themself to have any defect, and
judge everyone else to have had their mind seized. Therefore
hold onto this experiment before you, for it is of great virtue;
        but when   xx
you should wish that one to return to their prior, original state,
it can be done very well: On a Thursday, in the fifth hour of the night, go
to their door,[129] where the cloth is buried, which while it is buried
must be placed in a certain vessel so that it does not decay;
if you would make that one free and disinter that cloth,

---

129 Reading *ostium* for *hostium* in the ms.

[292r]

dicas O. Mẏrael. Oreoth. Pẏnen[130]. Otel. Trẏboẏ[131].
Norioch[132]. Belferich. Camoẏ. Ascaroth. Sobronoẏ
Sẏsmael. Ego talis absolvo vos ut eatis ad vestri
libitum, et relinquatis talem in statu priori: quibus
dictis fer tecum domum ipsum pannum, et accenso ligno olive,
et fenicla[133], et herbam berbenam propicias dictum pannum
super dicto[134] igne: dicendo sicut iste ignis consumit
hunc pannum, ita omnis ars per me facta contra talem
penitus consumetur: combusto igne proẏce dictum
pulverem in aqua currente, et omnis ars destructa   x
erit. Cognoscet, et se postea vir quod fuerit primo
omni praefectura privatu credens se habuisse
egritudinem cuius occasione hoc accessisse putabat[135]
et hoc est signum infrascriptum videlicet mẏrael:—

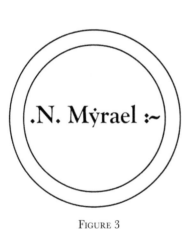

Figure 3

---

130 Cf. *Idinen* supra.

131 *Triay* in Clm 849 here, but not supra.

132 Cf. *Norẏoth* supra; *Moryoth* in Clm 849 here, but not supra.

133 *provincula* in Clm 849.

134 *...berbenam proicias dictum pannum sub dicto...* in Clm 849.

135 The text in Clm 849 ends at this point with "etcetera".

say thus: *O, Mirael, Oreoth, Pinen, Otel, Tryboy,*
Norioth, Belferich, Camoy, Ascaroth, Sobronoy,
Sysmael; I release you such that you may go at your
pleasure, and leave so and so in their prior state. These things
having been said, carry that cloth home with you, and lighting olive wood
and fennel[136] and the verbena herb, you shall cast[137] the aforesaid cloth
upon the aforesaid fire, saying: *Just as that fire consumes*
this cloth, so all the art performed by me against so and so
shall be consumed within. Having burned it in the fire, cast its
ashes into running water, and all the art   x
will be destroyed. That one will come to their senses, and afterwards shall be the
    person[138] that they were before
being deprived of every faculty, believing themself to have had
an illness to which they succumbed;
and here is the sign written below, namely of Mirael:

---

136 Reading *fenicula* for *fenicla* in the ms.

137 Reading *proicias* for *propicias* in the ms., as per Clm 849.

138 Literally, "the man".

[292v]

De odio, et inimicitia:—[139]

Restat etiam ut de odio, et inimicitia inter dilligentes
ponere pertractemus: Cum igitur inter viros sive
mulieres, sive masculum, et feminam seminare volueris inimicitiam aut odium capitale: necesse est
ut accipes duos lapides vivos, et recondes unius pon-
deris, qui debent esse fluminei: et in uno debes
sculpire nomen unius cum his nominibus scilicet carcuray[140].
mobabel. isobyl, et Geritaton[141]: et in altero nomen
alterius, et hec nomina scilicet puzavil, punaton. folficaẏ,   x
et mansator[142], quae nomina sunt valde se odientia.
Quibus sculptis quaeque videlicet est factus nomine unius debes[143]
sub ianua illius in limite[144] si potes subterrare:
si autem non sepelias sub limite cuiusdam domus inhabitate: et similiter alium sub limite eius, vel
alterius domus inhabitate, et ibidem stare permit-
tas septem diebus, et noctibus: quo facto ante solis
ortum removes, et in locum occultum ambos portes
et ipsos in ignem prohicias sic dicendo. Coniuro vos spiritus
inimicissimos per eterni dei Gloriam, et per quantum odium   xx
quod inter vos habetis[145] quod inter talem, et talem quorum
nomina in illis lapedibus sculpta permanent: quantum odium quod
inter vos est tantum, inter ipsos seminetis, et inseratis. Quibus ter dictis ipsos lapides de igne afferas
sic dicendo cum iraseretur furor eorum in nos fortisam
aqua absorbuisset nos: quo dicto proicias ipsos in aqua

---

139 cf. Clm 849, 13v-15r.

140 *carcurā* in the ms.

141 *Geritatō* in the ms.; the preceding names are rendered as *Cartutay*, *Momabel*, *Sobil*, and *Geteritacō* in Clm 849.

142 *Puzanil*, *Pimaton*, *Folfitoy*, and *Mansator* in Clm 849.

143 *...sculptis uni videlicet illum qui factus est nomine illius debes...* in Clm 849.

144 Likewise *limite* in Clm 849, however Kieckhefer amends this and the following instances as *limine*, "threshold".

145 *et per quantum odium quod inter vos habetis* omitted in Clm 849.

For Hatred and Ill Will

It yet remains
for us to investigate the laying of hatred and ill will between acquaintances.
　　When, therefore, between men or
women, or a male and a female,
you should wish to sow ill will or mortal hatred, it is necessary
that you take two uncut stones, and conceal one
of these, both of which must be taken from a river. And in one you must
carve the name of one of them, along with these names, which are Carcuray,
Mobabel, Isobyl, and Geritaton; and in the other, the name
of the other one, and these names, which are Puzavil, Punaton, Folficay,　　　x
and Mansator, which names are themselves exceedingly hateful.
These things having been carved — each one, that is, having been fashioned —
　　you must,
if possible, bury the name of one in the footpath beneath that one's doorway.
If, however, you cannot, then bury it beneath the footpath of some house
that you occupy; and likewise the other one beneath the other's footpath, or
that of another house you occupy; and there
you shall let them remain for seven days and nights. Which having been done,
　　before
sunrise remove them and carry both to a hidden place,
and cast them into a fire, saying thus: *I conjure you*
most hostile spirits by the eternal glory of God. And by as much hatred　　　xx
as you bear amongst yourselves, so much between such and such whose
names are carved in these stones shall be preserved; as much hatred as
there is amongst you, sow and
plant it between them. These things having thrice been said, bring forth those
　　stones from the fire,
saying thus: *When their fury at us was aggravated, perchance*
the water might have submerged us,[146] which having been said, cast them into water

---

146 Vulg. Ps. 123:3-4.

[293r]

frigidissima, et in ipsa stare permitte sereno caelo tribus diebus, et noctibus: quarto autem die accipies
ipsos, et suffumiga cum sulfure sic dicendo Coniuro
vos omnes demones odiosos, et malignos, invidos,
et discordes per unitatem spiritus sancti paracliti manen-
tis in patre, filio, et spiritu sancto: et per eternitatem omnes
creatoris: et per omnes sanctos, et sanctas dei: et per haec sancta
nomina, virtute quorum dominator olẏmpi caelum, et
terram est formare dignatus sua nomina. Sabaoth.
Helẏn, et tẏbatel[147]: et per omnes reges, et dominationes   x
inferni: et per hec nomina demonum, videlicet Apolẏn. Gebel
Ascaroth. Tereol. fulmar[148], et thẏroces. Quatenus
omne odium quod inter vos existit, et quantum odium inter
Chaim, et Abel fuit: tantum inter talem, et talem
protinus inseratis accendite: itaque ipsos et taliter
inflametis, quod unus alterum videre non valeat:
ymmo uno reliquum innumerabili odio rebelis
affligat: removeatur igitur ab ipsis omnis amor, di-
lectio, fraternitas compago, inimicitiam et odium
maximum convertantur. Quibus ter dictis suffu-   xx
migando ipsos semper reconde, nocte vero sequenti
collidas dictos lapides simul: et unum super reliquum
proicias sic dicendo, non collido hoc lapides: ẏmo
collido talem, et talem: quorum nomina hic sculpta sunt
quo unus alterum affligat perpetuo[149] odio se invicem

---

147 ...*dignatus scilicet Aa, Sabaoth, Helyn et Abacel* in Clm 849.

148 *fulmā* in the ms.; *Falmar* in Clm 849.

149 *immitigabili* in Clm 849.

most frigid, and let them remain there under a clear sky
for three days and nights; but on the fourth day take
them, and suffumigate them with sulfur, saying thus: *I conjure*
all of you demons, hateful and malicious, envious
and quarrelsome, by the unity of the holy spirit of the Paraclete,
subsisting in the Father, the Son, and the Holy Spirit; and by the eternity of all
things of the creator; and by all the sainted men and women of God; and by these holy
names, by virtue of which the ruler of Olympus
deigned to shape heaven and earth, with his names Sabaoth,
Helyn, and Tybatel; and by all the kings and dominions   x
of the infernal; and by these names of demons, which are Apolyn, Gebel,
Ascaroth, Tereol, Fulmar, and Thyroces. Insofar as
all the hatred that is amongst you exists, and as much hatred
as there was between Cain and Abel, so much
shall you plant between such and such forthwith. Ignite them, therefore, and so
inflame them that one cannot bear to see the other;
indeed,
one shall afflict the other with measureless, insurgent hatred. Therefore all love,
esteem, fraternity, and attachment shall be taken away,
turned to the greatest ill will and hatred. These things having thrice been said,   xx
continue to suffumigate them, then put them away; but the following night
you shall clash the aforesaid stones together, and
cast one upon the other, saying thus: *I do not clash stones here; rather*
I clash such and such, whose names are carved here
so that one shall afflict the other with perpetual hatred, each in turn

[293v]

de cetero trucident[150], et sic facias singula nocte, ac sin-
gulo die ter aliquis diebus: et videbis statim, sive audies quod inimici efficientur, et se oderint omnino: et unus alterum videre, non valebit. Si enim omnino ipsos disiungere
voles, et unum ab altero disgregare, et quod unus alterum
fugiat facias hoc modo: Surge die sabati ante solis
ortum decrescente luna, et maxime quando est in com-
bustione: et vade versus solis ortum, et versus solis
ortum foveam[151] facias. Qua facta habeas dictos lapides tecum
latos, et fortiter ipsos ad invicem collide pulsando   x
unum super alterum sic dicendo Non collido hos lapides
quo dicto ter sepelias quin volueris deinde recede
et versus occidentem vade, et fac foveam, et ibi sepelias dicendo sic Sicut disiunsi hos lapides, ita
talis se disiungat, a tali: et oppositi sint: sicut
isti lapides. Quo sepulto recede, et videbis illos
disiungi, et unum ab altero separari. Hoc experimentum occultandum est, quia ineffabilis in eo
virtus existit: nullum enim remedium invenitur
quando ipsi disiunguntur, et se mordaciter oderint. Cum   xx
vero volueris ad primam amicitiam remeare dese-
peliendi sunt praedicti lapides: et in fornace ponendi
qui bene cocti minutissime terrantur, et ipsos cum
aqua ad invicem impasta et siccare permitte. Quo
siccato in aqua fluminis prohicias dicendo. Tollatur

---

150 Kieckhefer reads *crucient* in Clm 849, but the scribal hand and use of contraction are sufficiently
    ambiguous to permit either interpretation.

151 *et versus solis ortum foveam* omitted in Clm 849.

savaging the other. And you shall do so each night and
each day for some three days, and at once you will see, or otherwise
hear, that they have become enemies, and absolutely hate each other, and one
cannot bear to see the other. If, however,
you should wish them to be parted completely, and one to be separated from the
    other, and that one
should flee the other, you shall work in this manner: Rise on a Saturday before
sunrise, the Moon waning, and especially while it is
combust, and turn toward the sunrise, and facing the
sunrise you shall make a hole in the ground. Which having been done, you shall
    take the aforesaid stones
you have carried with you, and forcefully clash them against each other,
    beating   x
one upon the other, saying thus: *I do not clash stones here*, etcetera,
which having thrice been said, you shall bury whichever one you wish, then
    withdraw
and turn toward the west, and make a hole in the ground, and in it
you shall bury the other, saying thus: *Just as I have separated these stones, thus
so and so shall be separated from so and so, and they shall be in opposition, just like
these stones.* Which having been buried, you shall withdraw, and you will see them
divided, and one separated from the other. This
experiment is to be kept secret, for there is ineffable
virtue in it; indeed, no remedy is to be found
once they are separated, and they shall hate bitingly.   xx
But when you wish to return them to their original friendship,
the aforesaid stones are disinterred and placed in an oven;
which stones, having been well cooked, are to be most finely ground, and
you shall mix them together with water and allow them to dry. Which
having been dried, you shall cast into running water, saying:

[294r]

omnis inimicitia, et ira quae fuit inter talem, et
talem: et in amorem pristinum revertantur per mi-
sericordiam pii dei, qui non respicit malitias pec-
catorum Amen: et scias quod hi statim coniunguntur,
et omnis ira tollitur et pristina pace fruuntur:—
    .Ut mulier non possit cognosci a, viro:—
Accipe acum virginem, et qui cum eo punxerit pedum dex-
trum mortui: et acumen illius acus scilicet punctam
posuerit in cullo illius scilicet in cenam: et mulier super
se portaverit non poterit cognosci a viro aliquo   x
modo:—
Item si quis talem acum posuerit sub pede suo dextro
existendo inter convivas, dum mensam sit primus qui
sedeat: et quando sub pede ponit dicat hec verba
Mane Tetel. alibi Tael phares: sciat pro certo quod
nullus poterit comedere dum pedem super acum
tenuerit: et si removerit pedem quo non ipsam super
acum teneat, bene poterunt comedere: et si postea posuerit iterum, iterum nullus comedere poterit
Finis:— et scies quod istud probatum per me Ale-   xx
xandrum:—

[294r]

All ill will and wrath which was between such and
such shall be taken away, and they shall return to their former love, by
the mercy of blessed God, who has no regard for the wickedness
of sinners, amen. And you shall know that they are at once united,
and all wrath is taken away and they enjoy the previous peace.

So That a Woman May Not Be Known By a Man

Take an unused pin, and with it puncture the
right foot of a corpse;[152] and the point of that pin — once having punctured,
    that is —
one shall place in the posterior of that woman — at the dinner table, that is —
    and the woman
bearing it upon herself shall not be able to be known[153] by a man by any   x
means.

Likewise, if one should place such a pin under one's right foot
while among dinner guests, before anyone is first
seated at the table, and say these words when one places it under one's foot:
Mane Tetel (or *Tael*) *Phares*,[154] one shall know for certain that
no one will be able to eat while one's foot
remains upon the pin; and if one should remove one's foot so that it does not
remain upon the pin, everyone will be able to eat well. And if
afterwards one should put it there again, again no one will be able to eat.
The end. And you will know that this has been tested by me,   xx
Alexander.[155]

---

152 Popular belief in the magical and medicinal properties of corpses – especially those of criminals – persisted well into the modern era (see Davies & Matteoni, 2017); however, I have yet to discover any other reference to practices comparable to this particular ritual.

153 The possible connotations of *cognosci* encompass recognition, acquaintance, etc., but given the context and the typical proclivities of magical texts, knowledge of the carnal sort may be implied.

154 See Daniel 5:25-28.

155 While it is tempting to infer from the placement of this postscript within the colophon that we have here the name of our scribe, the perfunctory and mechanical rendering of the name itself (broken across two lines, with the final *m* suspended in the ms.) suggests that it, too, was copied from an exemplar text.

[294v]

Experimentum Michaelis Scoti nigromantici.
Si volueris per demones habere scientiam qui in forma magistri ad te veniet cum tibi placuverit expedit tibi
primo habere quandam cameram fulgentem, et nitidam in
qua numquam mulier non conversetur: nec vir ante   x
inchoationem triginta diebus computato itaque tem-
pore taliter quod xxxi. die: sit luna crescens Mercurius[156]
eius hora, castus per septimanam: rasus totus, ac etiam
lotus, nec non vestimentis albis indutus. Solus
in ortu solis, in quo et ipsam hora Mercurii habeas quod-
dam vas in quo sic lignum aloes, camphora, et cipres-
sum cum igne: ex quibus fiet fumus: et primo
te totum suffumiga scilicet primo faciem, deinde alia:

---

156 As per Boudet and Véronèse, 2012; ♆ in the ms.

An Experiment of Michael Scot, Necromancer

If you should wish to have knowledge by demons, who in the form of a teacher
will come to you when it should please you, it is advantageous for you
first of all to have some chamber, pristine and neat, in
which neither woman nor man ever dwelt. Before   x
beginning, you shall account for thirty days,
such that it is thus the thirty-first day; with the Moon waxing,
in the hour of Mercury, having been chaste for a week; fully shaved, and also
bathed, nor without having donned white vestments, alone,
at sunrise, when it is also the hour of Mercury, you shall take
a certain vessel in which aloeswood, camphor, and cypress
are put to the flame, from which smoke is produced; and first
of all, you should suffumigate yourself entirely — first your face, that is, then
    the rest —

[295r]

postea etiam totam cameram. Quo facto habeas oleum bacharum, et
totum te ungue a, capite usque ad pedes: hoc facto volve te primo versus Sol ortum et sic dic flexis genibus O, admirabilis, et ineffabilis, et incomprehen-
sibilis, qui omnia ex nihilo formasti: apud quem nihil
impossible est, te deprecor cum humilitate vehemen-
ti ut mihi famulo tuo tali tribuas gratiam cogno-
scendi potentiam tuam qui vivis, et regnas cum deo patre
per omnia secula seculorum amen. Presta quesummus mi-
hi tutellam angeli tui qui me custodiat, protegat   x
atque defendat, et adiuvet ad huius operis consuma-
tionem et faciat me potentem contra omnes spiritus ut
vincam, etiam dominer eis: et ipsi adversus me
terrendi, ut ledendi nullam habeant potestatem
amen. Adhesit pavimento anima mea secundum ver-
bum tuum scilicet vias meas anuntiavi et exaudisti me,
doce me iustificationes tuas viam: iustificationum
tuarum instrue me, et exercebor in mirabilibus
tuis: Dormitavit anima mea prae tedio confirma me
in verbis tuis amen. Similiter versus occasum, me-   xx
ridiem, et septentrionem: et debes scire quod quando vertis
te debes te totum expoliare nudum, deinde dicere
has orationes: quo facto debes te induere dicendo hunc psalmum. Notus in iudea deus, usqe
quoniam cogitatio hominis etc. quo dicto, et inducto dic-

[295r]

then the whole chamber as well. Which having been done you shall take olive
    oil and
anoint every part of yourself with it, from head to feet; this having been done,
first you shall turn to face the risen Sun, and thus on bended knees say:
O, admirable, and ineffable, and incomprehensible;
who has fashioned everything from nothing, before whom nothing
is impossible, ardently and humbly to you I pray
that to me your servant you may grant the grace which is known
to be in the power of you who live and reign with God the Father
for all the ages of ages, amen. I beg you lend to me
the guardianship of an angel of yours who shall guard, protect   x
and defend me, and be of help in the completion of this work,
and make me able to prevail against all spirits,
and even to rule them; and them to be in fear before me,
so that none have the power to do harm,
amen. My soul has cleaved to the dust; give me life, according to
your word. For I have confessed my ways, and you have heard me;
teach me your justifications. Instruct me in the way of your reasons,
and I will take part in your wonders.
My soul has slumbered because of weariness; strengthen me
in your words, amen.[157] Likewise facing west, south,   xx
and north; and you must know that as you turn about
you must be entirely stripped bare, thereafter saying
those orations. Which having been done you must take it upon yourself to recite
this psalm: *In Judea God is known*, up to
For the thinking of man, etcetera.[158] Which having been said, and conducted,

---

157 Lines 15-20 comprise Vulg. Ps. 118:25-29, but the scribe's omissions and interpolations render
    it somewhat nonsensical. The Sixto-Clementine version of 1592, which closely approximates
    the text from which the scribe was evidently working and is used for the present translation,
    reads:
        Adhæsit pavimento anima mea; vivifica me secundum verbum tuum.
        Vias meas enuntiavi, et exaudisti me; doce me justificationes tuas.
        Viam justificationum tuarum instrue me, et exercebor in mirabilibus tuis.
        Dormitavit anima mea præ tædio; confirma me in verbis tuis.

158 Vulg. Ps. 75:2-11.

[295v]

ter hec verba Os iusti meditabur sapientiam, et lingua
eius loquetur iuditium: Quibus dictis habeas unum frustrum
panni albi de lana quae numquam fuerit in usu, et habeas
quandam columbam albam totam ut -o-[159] cuiuscumque coloris
sit, et trunca eius collum, et collige sanguine in vase
vitreo: et de dicta columba sive cor[160] auffer sangui-
nando dictum cor in <ꙮ.o.> fac cum dicto corde cruentato
in dicto panno circulum, ut apparet inferius: quo facto
intra circulum cum ense in manu: qui ensis debet
esse lucidissimus, cum quo ense avis capud debet   x
truncari ut dictum est: et ipsum tenendo per cuspidem
aspiciendo versus orientem dic sic. O. misericordis-
sime deus creator omnium, et omnium scientiarum largitor:
qui vis magis peccatorem vivere, ut ad penitent-
tiam valeat pervenire quam ipsum mori sordidum in pec-
catis: te deprecor toto mentis affectu, ut cogas
et liges istos tres demones videlicet Appolyn, Maraloch,
Berich, ut debeant per virtutem, et potentiam tuam
mihi obedire, servire, et parere sine aliquo fraude,
malignatione, ut furore in omnibus quae praecipio: qui   xx
vivis, et regnas in unitate spiritus sancti Amen:
Debet haec enim oratio dici novies versus orientem, deinde debes dicere. Appolyn. Maraloch. Berich. Ego
talis vos exorcizo, et coniuro ex parte dei omnipoten-
tis, qui vos vestra elatione[161] iussit antra subire pro-

---

159 I have been unable to determine what, if any, significance this notation bears.

160 Appended by superscript over another -o- in the ms.

161 *electione* in Clm 849.

these words shall be said: *The mouth of the just will contemplate wisdom, and his tongue will speak judgment.*[162] Having said these things, you shall take a piece of white wool cloth that has never been used, and you shall take a certain dove, entirely white — or of whatsoever color it may be — and cut its throat, and collect the blood in a vessel of glass; and concerning the aforesaid dove, or rather its heart, you shall remove, still bleeding, the aforesaid heart <in one stroke>.[163] Make with the aforesaid heart a bloody circle in the aforesaid cloth, as appears below.[164] Which having been done you shall enter the circle with a sword in hand, which sword must be most bright, with which sword the bird's head must   x be cut off as has been said; and holding it by the blade, looking toward the east you shall say thus: *O, most merciful God, creator of everything, and bestower of all knowledge; who wishes rather that the sinner live, that he may be able to come to repentance, than he die soiled in sin: I pray to you with all the feeling of my mind, that you may compel and bind those three demons, namely Appolyn, Maraloch, and Berich, that they shall by your virtue and power obey, serve, and submit to me without any fraud, malice, or rage in all that I command; you who*   xx *live and reign in the undivided Holy Spirit, amen.* Verily this oration must be spoken nine times facing east, then you must say: *Appolyn, Maraloch, Berich, I so exorcize and conjure you on behalf of omnipotent God, who commanded you according to your office to enter deep tombs,*

---

162 Vulg. Ps. 36:30.

163 Conjectural reading of *i°.o.* in the ms.

164 Fig. 4, 297r; cf. Clm 849, 4v. The inscription "fulomon" is most likely a scribal error for "nomen"; however, it is conceivable that the author actually recorded the name of a spirit he encountered in performing this experiment.

[296r]

fundi ut debeatis mittere quendam spiritum peritum dog-
mate omnium scientiarum qui mihi sit benivolus, fidelis,
et placidus ad docendum omnem scientiam quam voluero
veniens.[165] veniens in formam magistri ut nullam for-
midinem percipere valeam fiat, fiat, fiat. Item
coniuro vos per patrem, et filium, et spiritum sanctum,
et per haec sancta nomina quorum virtute ligamen scilicet Dobel,
Uriel, Sabaoth. Semonẏ, Adonaẏ, Tetragramaton.
Albumaẏzi. Loch. Morech. Sadabẏn. Rodobel.
Donnel. Parabẏel. Alatuel. <Nominam>[166], et Usobel.   x
Quatenus vos tres reges maximi, et mihi sotii
mihi petenti unum de subditis vestris mitterere labo-
retis qui sit magister omnium scientiarum, et artium veniens
in forma humana placibilis aplaudens mihi, et
erudens me cum amore ita, et taliter quod in termino xxx.[ta] dierum talem scientiam valeam adipisci
promittens post sumptionem scientiae dare sibi licen-
tiam recedendi, ut hoc etiam totiens dici debet haec
oratione vero dicta ense depone, et involve in
dicto panno: et facto vasiculo[167] cuba super ipso ut ali-   xx
quantulum dormias, post sompnum vero surge, et in-
duas te: quia facto vasiculo[168] homo se spoliat, et
intrat cubiculum ponendo dictum vasiculum super capite[169]. Est autem sciendum quod dictis his coniurationibus
somnus acculit[170] virtute divina, in sompno autem

---

165 sic.

166 *Noiam* in the ms.

167 *fasciculo* in Clm 849.

168 *fasciculo* in Clm 849.

169 *fasciculum sub capite* in Clm 849.

170 *accidit* in Clm 849.

[296r]

that you must send a certain dead spirit bearing the doctrine
of all sciences, who shall benevolently, faithfully,
and peacefully teach me all the knowledge that I will wish,
approaching in the form of a teacher so that I
shall feel no fear; let it be done, let it be done, let it be done. Just as
I conjure you by the Father, and the Son, and the Holy Spirit;
and by these holy names whose virtue is a bond, namely Dobel,
Uriel, Sabaoth, Semony, Adonay, Tetragrammaton,
Albumaïzi, Loch, Morech, Sadabyn, Rodobel,
Donnel, Parabïel, Alatuel, Nominam, and Usobel,   x
so you three great kings, and my companions,
I desire that you endeavor to have one who is subject to you sent to me,
who shall be a master of all sciences and arts, coming
to me in a human form, pleasantly applauding, and
thus teaching me with love; and so that within
thirty days such knowledge I shall be able to obtain,
promising after having acquired that knowledge to give that one license
to withdraw, as indeed this must so often be said. This
oration verily having been said, put aside the sword, and wrap it in
the aforesaid cloth; and having made the bundle, you shall lie atop it as if   xx
to sleep. After sleeping, verily you shall rise, and dress
yourself; for having made the bundle, one unwraps it and
enters the bedchamber, placing the aforesaid bundle under one's
head.[171] But it is to be known that having said these conjurations,
sleep descends[172] by a divine virtue; but in sleep

---

171 Reading *fasciculo* for all instances of *vasiculo* in ll. 20-23 of the ms., and *sub capite* for *super capite*
    in ll. 23-24, as per Clm 849.

172 Reading *accidit* for *acculit* in the ms., as per Clm 849.

[296v]

apparebunt tibi tres maximi reges cum famulis in-
numeris militibus, peditibus: inter quos est etiam
quidam magister apparens, cui ipsi tres reges iubent
ad te ipsum venire paratam. Videbis enim tres reges
fulgentes mira pulcritudine, qui tibi in dicto sompno viva voce loquentur dicentes. Ecce tibi damus
quod multotiens postulasti, et dicent illi magistro
sit iste tuus discipulus quem docere tibi Iube-
mus omnem scientiam, sive artem quam audire volu-
erit. Doce illum taliter, et erudi, ut in termino   x
xxx. dierum in qualem scientiam voluerit ut summus inter
alios habeatur: et ipsum audies, et videbis eum respondere dictum mei libentissime faciam quicquid
vultis. His dictis reges abibunt, et magister
solus remanebit: qui tibi dicet surge, ecce
tuus magister. His vero dictis excitaberis statim et aperi-
es occulos, et videbis quendam magistrum optime
indutum: qui tibi dicet, da mihi ensem quem sub
capite tenes. Tu vero dices ecce discipulus
vester paratus est facere quicquid vultis: tamen   xx
debes habere pugillarem, et scribere omnia quae tibi
dicet. Primo debes querere o, magister quod est
nomen vestrum ipse dicet, et tu scribes: Secundo de
quo ordine, et similiter scribe: his scriptis dabis
ensem quo habito ipse recedet, dicens expecta me

will appear to you three great kings with innumerable handmaidens,
and soldiers on foot; among whom also
a certain magister is to be seen, whom those three kings command
be prepared to come to you. Indeed you will see three kings
shining with marvelous beauty, who in the aforesaid slumber
will speak to you, saying: "Behold, we give to you
that which many times you have requested", and they will say to the magister:
"That one shall be your student whom we command you to teach
every science or art that he may wish to hear.
You shall teach and educate him such that within   x
thirty days, in such knowledge as he shall have wished,
he shall be held as the greatest among all others." And [to you they will say]:
    "You will listen to him, and see him answer
our command most willingly, performing whatever
you wish." These things having been said, the kings will depart, and the
    magister
alone remain, who will say to you: "Rise, behold
your teacher." But these things having been said, you will at once awaken and
    open
your eyes, and see a certain magister, very well
dressed, who will say to you: "Give me the sword which
you keep under your head." But you will say: *Behold, your student*
is prepared to do whatever you wish. Yet   xx
you must have a tablet, and write all that
he says to you. First you must ask: *O, magister, what is*
your name? He will say, and you will write. Second: *Of*
which order? And likewise you shall write. These things having been written, you
    will surrender
the sword, having which he will withdraw, saying: "Wait for me

donec veniam, tu nihil dices magister vero recedet
et secum portabit ensem, post cuius recessum tu
solves pannum, ut apparet inferius: etiam scribes
in dicto circulo nomen eius scriptum per te, et
scribi debet etiam cum supradicto .O.[173] quo scripto involve dictum pannum, et bene reconde: his factis debes prandere solo pane, et pura aqua:
et illa die non egredi cameram, et cum pransus
fueris accipe pannum, et intra circulum versus
Appollÿm[174], et dic sic o rex apolÿn[175] magne   x
potens, et venerabilis: ego famulus tuus in
te credens, et omnio confidens quia tu es fortior, et
valens per incomprehensibilem maiestatem tuam:
ut famulus, et subditus tuus talis magister meus
debeat ad me venire quam citius fieri potest per
virtutem et potentiam tuam quae est magna, et
maxima in secula, seculorum amen. Et similiter
dicere versus Maraloth[176]
mutando nomen: et versus
Berith[177] similiter: his dictis acci-   xx
pe de dicto sanguine, et scri-
be in circulo nomen tuum cum
supradicto corde, ut hic apparet inferius. Deinde scribe
cum dicto corde in angulis panni

Figure 4

---

173 *sanguine* in Clm 849.

174 sic.

175 sic.

176 sic.

177 sic.

until I shall come"; you will say nothing. Verily the magister will withdraw
and take the sword with him, after which withdrawal you
will unfold the cloth, as appears below, and you will write
in the aforesaid circle the name of him that you wrote, and
it must be written, furthermore, with the aforesaid blood,[178] Which having been
    written
you shall wrap up the aforesaid cloth, and hide it well. These things having been
    done,
you must break fast on only bread and pure water,
and not exit the chamber that day; and when
you have finished breakfast you shall take the cloth, and enter the circle facing
Appolyn, and say thus: *O King Appolyn, great,*   x
powerful, and venerable: I, your servant,
trust in you, and have absolute confidence that you are brave, and
strong in your incomprehensible majesty;
so a distinguished servant and subject of yours, my teacher,
must come to me, which is made possible sooner by
the virtue and power of you who are great and
supreme unto the ages of ages, amen. And say likewise
facing Maraloch,
having changed the name, and facing
Berich likewise. These things having been said, you shall take   xx
the aforesaid blood, and write in the circle your name with
the heart mentioned likewise, as appears
here below. Then write
with the aforesaid heart in the corners of the cloth

---

178 Reading *sanguine* for *.O.*, per Clm 849.

illa nomina, ut hic apparent. Si autem sanguis unius
avis non tibi sufficeret, potes interficere quod tibi pla-
cent: quibus omnibus factis sedebis per totum diem in circulo aspiciens ipsum nihil loquendo: cum vero sero fuerit
plica dictum pannum spoliato, et intra cubiculum ponendo ipsum sub capite tuo: et cum posueris, dici sic plana
voce O, Appolÿn, Maraloch, Berich. Sathan. Belÿal
Belzebuth. Lucifer. Supplico vobis ut precipitatis
magistro meo nominando eius nomen ut ipse debeat
venire solus ante cras ad me[179]: et docere me talem
scientiam sine aliqua alia fallatia per illum qui venturus est
iudicare vivos, et mortuos, et seculum per ignem amen.
Cave igitur, et praecave ne signum ✠ facias propter magnum periculum: In sompno scies quia videbis magistrum
tota nocte loqui tecum interrogans a te qualem scientiam vis
adiscere, et tu dices talem: Itaque ut dictus est tota
nocte, cum eo loquentis. Cum itaque excitatus fueris in ipsa
nocte surge, et accende candelam, et accipe dictum pannum, et dissolve, et sede in eo scilicet in circulo ubi nomen tuum scriptum est ad tuum commodum, et voca nomen
magistri tui sic dicens, O, talis de talis ordine in magistrum meum datum per maiores reges tuos te deprecor
ut venies in forma benigna ad docendum me in
tali scientia quia sim probior omnibus mortalibus do-
cens ipsam cum magno gaudio sine aliquo labore

    x

    xx

---

179 ...*venire cras ante Solis ortum ad me* in Clm 849.

those names as here appear. If, however, the blood of one
bird shall not suffice for you, you can kill as many as you
please. All of this having been done, you will sit for a whole day in the circle,
inspecting[180] it, saying nothing; but when the hour has become late
you shall fold the aforesaid cloth, undress, and entering the bedchamber place
it under your head. And when you have placed it, speak thus in a firm
voice: *O, Appolyn, Maraloch, Berich, Sathan, Belïal,*
Belzebuth, Lucifer, I beseech you all that you shall enjoin
my teacher (who is to be identified by his name), *that he must*
come to me, alone, before tomorrow,[181] *and teach me such*   x
knowledge without any deceit at all; by he who is coming
to judge the living, and the dead, and the world by fire, amen.
So beware, and take heed that you do not make the sign ✠, for it is of great
peril. In sleep you will know wherefore you keep watch for the magister,
all night speaking with you, asking you what sort of knowledge you wish
to audit, and you saying as much; and so just as it is said,
speaking with him all night. Therefore when you have awoken that
night you shall rise, and light a candle, and take the aforesaid
cloth, and unfold it, and sit there, that is to say in the circle where
your name is written, at your convenience, and call the name   xx
of your teacher, saying thus: *O, so and so, of such and such order,*
given as my teacher by your superior kings, I pray you
come in a pleasant form to instruct me in
such knowledge, wherefore I shall be taught it better than all mortals,
with great delight, without any labor,

---

180 cf. the meditative *inspicio* of notae in the *Ars notoria* (Skemer, 2010: 151).

181 Or, "come to me tomorrow before sunrise" as per Clm 849.

[298r]

ac omni tedio derelicto. Veni igitur ex tuorum parte
maioris qui regnant per infinita secula seculorum amen.
fiat, fiat fiat. Hiis itaque dictis ter[182] aspicias versus occidentem videbis magistrum venire cum multis
discipulis quem rogabis ut omnes abire iubeat, et
statim recedent: quo facto ipse magister dicet quam
scientiam audire desideras tu dices talem, et tunc in-
cipies: memento enim quia tantum adiscens memoriae commo-
dabis, et omnem scientiam quam habere volueris adisces in termino
xxx. dierum. Et quando ipsum de camera abire vo-   x
lueris, plica pannum et reconde, et statim recedet: et quando
ipsum venire volueris aperi pannum, et subito ibidem ap-
parebit continuando lectiones. Post vero terminum
xxx. dierum dictus optime in illa scientiam evades, et fac
tibi dare ensem tuum: et dic ut vadat, et cum pace
recedat. Debes iterum dicere cum pro alia ipsum
invocabis habenda scientia, quod tibi dicet ad tuum libitum
esse parratum. Finis capituli scientiae. Explicit ni-
cromantiae experimentum illustrissimi doctoris domini magistri Michaelis Scoti, qui summus inter alios nominatur   xx
magister qui fuit Scotus, et servus praeclarissimo domino suo
domino philipo regis Ceciliae coronato, quod destinavit
sibi dum esset aegrotus in civitate Cordube, etcetera. Finis:—

---

182 *tunc* in Clm 849.

[298r]

and all tedium forsaken. Come, therefore, from your
high place which you rule for endless ages of ages, amen.
Let it be done, let it be done, let it be done. And so, those things having thrice been
    said, look[183]
toward the east and see the magister approaching with many
students, all of whom you will ask him to order to depart, and
at once they will withdraw; which having been done that teacher will speak as
    much
of such knowledge as you say you wish to hear, and then you will
begin. Indeed you shall remember it, for as much as is learned your memory
shall accommodate, and every science you should wish to have you will learn
    within
thirty days. And when you wish him to depart the   x
chamber, you shall fold up the cloth and put it away, and at once he will
    withdraw; and when
you wish him to come you shall unfold the cloth, and suddenly he will appear
and continue the lectures. But after
thirty days, you will have been most excellently instructed in that knowledge;
    and you shall have
your sword given to you, and say that he shall go, and peacefully
withdraw. You must call again when
you would invoke him to have some other knowledge, which
he is prepared to expound to you at your pleasure. Here ends this chapter of
    science. Thus is unfolded
the necromantic experiment of the most renowned doctor, lord magister
    Michael
Scot, who is called the greatest master among all others;   xx
who was a Scot, and servant of his most famed master,
Lord Philip, cleric[184] of the king of Sicily; which experiment he resolved to
    undertake
while he was ill in the city of Cordoba, etcetera. The end.

---

183 Or, "having been said, then look" as per Clm 849.

184 *coronato*, i.e. tonsured; see Brown, 1897: 19.

[303r]

In ratione cursu velocissimo in parva hora habet omnes lectiones 66. sub suo modo, vel habet 60. legiones:

Avedie rex et dux magnus apparet corronatis dẏademate, nihilo videtur de eo nisi caput: et ante eum procedunt ministri duo ferentes tubas. Docet ad plenum loẏcam, et hẏcam et omni perenni dat artes optime intellectus omnium linguarum. Dat optimos familiares. Dat ad plenum vera responsa de presentis, praeteritis, et futuris de artibus, ut rebus occulte consecratis: x
et archanis, et secretis: et de consecratione eorum, et de lapsu, et qualiter peccaverunt: et non per horam stat inveritate nisi intromittatur intus angulum: et tunc dat vera responsa de omnibus interrogantibus. 30. legiones:

Habet 40. legiones.

Boab magnus preses apparet in similitudinem militis, caput eius assimmilatur Leoni: equitat super equum magnum, nigrum: eius oculi resplendent sicut flamma: Loquitur rauca voce, et habet magnos dentes. Dat optime omni naturalium intellectum   xx
atque latratus canum: et transferre argentum, et aurum de loco ad locum. Dat ad plenum vera responsa de rebus occultis, et de omnibus interrogantibus presentibus, praeteritis, et futuris. Habet 40. legiones:

On the Method of Proceeding Most Quickly, in a Short Time, to Have All Sixty-Six Conscripts Subject to One's Terms, or To Have Sixty Legions

Avedie, a great king and duke, appears crowned with a
diadem, nothing to be seen of him except his head; and before him
proceed two ministers carrying trumpets. He teaches all of
logic and rhetoric,[185] and at all times gives the skills to
understand all languages excellently. He gives very good familiars.
He gives full, true answers about things present, past, and
future concerning the arts, or things consecrated in secret,   x
and things intimate and hidden, and of the consecration of these;
and of the Fall, and how they sinned. And not for an hour
does he stay truthful unless sent into an angled figure,[186]
and then he gives true answers concerning all inquiries. Thirty legions.

    Having 40 legions

Boab, a great president, appears in the likeness of a
soldier, his head like that of a lion; he rides upon
a great black horse; his eyes glitter
like flame. He speaks with a harsh voice, and has big
teeth. He gives excellent understanding of all things natural,   xx
even the barking of dogs, and he transfers silver and gold
from place to place. He gives full, true answers about
hidden things, and all inquiries
concerning things present, past, and future. He has forty legions.

---

185 Conjectural reading of *loȳcam, et hȳcam*.

186 *intus angulum*, possibly "into a corner".

[303v]

Habet 26. legiones.

Bille dux fortis apparet in similitudinem draconis, habet tria
capita quorum tertium assimilatur homini: et loquitur
rauca voce, et facit corporea mortuorum de loco,
ad locum scilicet transmutari: et suos demones super sepul-
crum apparere, et congregare: et facit hominem locupletem
in omnibus divitiis. Et facit ipsum loquentem, et sapientes
dant vera responsa omnibus interrogantibus: habet
sub se .26. legiones:

Habet .26 legiones, partim de ordine Troni, et partim de ordine angellorum

x

Fameis vel fronone similis marchio magnus apparet in multitudine: et facit hominem mirabilem
in Rectoricha. Dat optimos familiares. Intellectus
linguarum, et gratiam homini amicorum, et inimicorum: habet
.26. sub se, partim de ordine Troni, et partim de
ordine angellorum:

Habet 20. legiones.

Beduch ut bamone magnus marchio apparet in
similitudinem leopardi: habet alas ad modum Griffonis,
sed cum suscipit formam humanam dat optime amorem
mulierum: et facit eas languescere, febricitare in
amorem alicuius si sibi iunctum fiunt, libenter pandit
secreta mulierum, et deridet eas si sibi visum fiunt: et
facit spolioni, et nudus ludere luxuriose. Dat fa-
cundiam, et habet 20. legiones sub suo dominio:

xx

[303v]

Having 26 legions

Bille, a strong duke, appears in the likeness of a dragon having three
heads, of which the third is like that of a man, and he speaks
with a harsh voice; and no doubt he causes bodies of the dead
to be shifted from place to place, and their spirits
to appear over each one's tomb, and to congregate; and he makes one wealthy
in all riches. And he makes those spirits speak, and the wise
to give true answers to all inquiries. He has
twenty-six legions under him.

Having 26 legions, partly of the order of Thrones, and partly of the order of Angels

Fameis, or **Fronone**, appears in a crowd in the likeness of a great   x
marquis; and he makes one marvelous
in rhetoric. He gives very good familiars, understanding
of languages, and the goodwill of friends as well as enemies. He has
twenty-six [legions] under him, partly of the order of Thrones, and partly of
the order of Angels.

Having 20 legions

Beduch, or **Bamone**, a great marquis, appears in
the likeness of a leopard; he has wings in the manner of a griffon,
but assuming a human form he excellently grants the love
of women, and makes them faint, feverish with   xx
love for anyone to whom they are attached; he eagerly reveals
the secrets of women, and laughs at them if they are seen by him; and
he makes them strip, and play luxuriously in the nude. He gives
eloquence, and has twenty legions under his dominion.

[304r]

Habet 19. legiones.

Bonoreae magnus marchio et dux apparet in similitudinem monstri. Facit hominem mirabilem in
Rectoricha: Dat optime intellectus omnium linguarum.
Dat gratiam amicorum, et inimicorum: et habet 19. legiones sub suo dominio:

Habet 26. Legiones.

Nunc autem dicendum est de Berich, Berich autem Rex est
et dux magnus inter omnibus vocatur Salamonazi
vocant ipsum hoc nomine Berich: Gramatii vero Belfaẏt,　　　　x
Apparet in similitudinem militis rubei, et eius equus
rubeus est: et indumenta eius rubea sunt, et est
coronatus duplici corona. Dat ad plenum vera responsa de praeteritis, presentibus, et futuris: cogitur virtute divina, et per annulum magice aris: sed ad libe-
ralem, mendax est: Docet ad plenum omnia genera me-
tallorum transferre in aurum, et argentum. Dat di-
gnitatem, et confirmat clarum intellectum: raucam
habet vocem, et habet sub se .26. legiones:

Ascaroth dux magnus, et fortis apparet in angelica　　　　xx
forma, ut spiratione turpissima, equitat super infernalem
Draconem: in dextra fert viperam. Dat ad plenum vera
responsa de presentibus, praeteritis, et futuris: de occultis rebus libenter loquitur: de sacratione, et eorum
lapsu: et qualiter peccaverunt, et reciderunt in spebus

Having 19 legions

Bonoreae, a great marquis and duke, appears in the likeness
of a monster. He makes one wonderful in
rhetoric. He gives excellent understanding of all languages.
He gives the goodwill of friends as well as enemies, and has nineteen legions
under his dominion.

Having 26 legions

But now we are to speak of **Berich**. Berich, although
called a king and a great duke among the masses, the Solomonists
call him by this name Berich; the grammarians, **Belfayt**.   x
He appears in the likeness of a red soldier, and his horse
is red; and his garments are red, and he is
crowned with a double crown. He gives full, true answers
about things past, present, and future, being compelled by
divine virtue, and by a ring of magical art; but at
liberty, he is deceitful. He teaches everything about
transforming all species of metals into gold and silver. He gives
dignity, and strengthens clarity of intellect;
he has a harsh voice, and has twenty-six legions under him.

Ascaroth, a great and strong duke, appears in an angelic   xx
form, though his breath is most vile, riding upon an infernal
dragon; in his right hand he carries a viper. He gives full, true
answers about things present, past, and future;
he speaks eagerly of secret things, of consecration; and of their
Fall, and how they sinned, and abandoned hope.

cecidisse mirabiliter reddunt hominem in omnibus
liberalibus artibus. Cavendum est unicuique exorciste
ab isto ascharoth, nec dimittat ipsum sibi apropinquare
quom intollerabilem fetorem ab ore eius prohicit: et
agreditur in defecto immensus: idcirco cavendum est
sibi ne superveniat, teneat igitur exorcista se audaciter
et suffumigatur sandalis:

Habet .29. legiones.

Foreas, ut fortas, ut sartas preses magnus apparet
in similitudinem ursi fortissimi humanam formam. Co-   x
gnoscit vires herbarum, et lapidum preciosorum. Docet
ad plenum practicam loices, et earum partes:
reddit hominem invisibilem, ingeniosum, eloquentem
vehementem, habet .29. legiones:

Habet xxv. legiones:

Furfur magnus comes, Apparet in similitudinem
corvi: cauda eius, sicut flamma: mendax est omnibus
nisi intromittatur inter angulum: sed cum ibi fuerit
suscipit angelicam formam, Loquitur rauca voce:
et ductor est armorum inter viros et mulieres reddit.   xx
Reddit homines invisibiles. Dat astronomiam
in omnibus artibus mecaneis. Dat intellectum produ-
cit fulgura, coruscationes, et tonitrua illas partes
si sibi fiunt: Scit optime respondere de occultis rebus, et habet sub se 25. legiones:

Having fallen, they marvelously restore to one all of
the liberal arts. Every exorcist is to beware
of that one Ascaroth, nor shall one permit him to approach oneself
while he discharges that intolerable stench from his mouth and
advances in immense rebellion; for this reason beware that
he not overcome you. Therefore the exorcist shall fearlessly keep a grip on
    himself
and be suffumigated with sandalwood.
    Having 29 legions
Foreas, or **Fortas**, or **Sartas**, a great president, appears
in the likeness of a mighty bear with a human form. He knows   x
the powers of herbs, and of precious stones. He teaches
all of practical logic, and the parts thereof;
he renders one invisible, ingenious, eloquent,
and ardent; he has twenty-nine legions.
    Having 25 legions
Furfur, a great count, appears in the likeness
of a crow, its tail like fire; he is deceitful in all things
unless sent into an angled figure, but once he is there
he assumes an angelic form, speaking in a harsh voice;
and he is a commander of arms among men, and delivers women.   xx
He renders people invisible. He teaches astronomy
among all the mechanical arts. He gives understanding of how
lightning, flashes, and thunder are produced in those places
where they are supposed to be made. He knows how best to answer concerning
    secret
matters, and has twenty-five legions under him.

[305r]

De ordine dominationum, habet 30 legiones:
Margoas, ut Margodas, ut Mardoas, ut Margutas magnus marchio apparet in similitudinem lupi fortissimi, cauda eius serpentina. Caudam ex ore proicit,
et cum suscipit humanam formam ductor est Armorum
et pugnator optimus. Dat ad plenum vera responsa de omnibus interrogatis: et est fidelis in omnibus mandatis exorciste: fuit de ordine dominationum: habet sub sua potestate 30. legiones: et spectat
post 1200. annos remeare, quod non est credendum: x

Habet 20. legiones:
Alphas ut Malapas preses magnus Apparet in
similitudinem corvi, sed cum suscipit formam humanam loquitur rauca voce. Mirabiliter edificat domos, et turres: et cito dat occursum maximos
artifices: facit etiam exorcistam res domos destruere, et
turres frangere. Dat optimos familiares ad
destructionem libenter suscipit sacrificia, holocausta: et decipit homines in violantes sibi
habet sub se 20. legiones: xx

Habet 12. legiones. Fuit de ordine virtutum
Gorsor, ut Gorson dux fortis apparet in similitudinem
hominis, caput eius assimilatur nocticorati: Mirabiliter
reddit hominem in phitonicha arte facit homines coa-
dunare coram exorcista quam ipse est penator penarum: quae
sunt <externis>, ut extremis partibus omnes homicide in

Of the order of Dominions, having 30 legions

Margoas, or **Margodas**, or **Mardoas**, or **Margutas**, a great
marquis, appears in the likeness of a
mighty wolf, the tail of which is serpentine. Casting the tail from his mouth,
and assuming a human form, he is a commander of arms
and an excellent fighter. He gives full, true answers
concerning everything you ask, and he is trustworthy in all
that the exorcist commands. He was of the order of
Dominions; he has thirty legions under his power, and he endeavors
after twelve hundred years to return, which is not to be believed.   x

Having 20 legions

Alphas, or **Malapas**, a great president, appears in
the likeness of a crow, but assuming a human
form he speaks with a harsh voice. He marvelously builds
houses and towers, and quickly grants a meeting with the greatest
artificers; likewise he causes the exorcist to destroy houses, and
to shatter towers. He gives very good familiars for
destruction. He eagerly receives sacrifices and burnt
offerings, and he tricks people into harming themselves.
He has twenty legions under him.   xx

Having 12 legions; formerly of the order of Virtues

Gorsor, or **Gorson**, a strong duke, appears in the likeness
of a man, his head like that of a night raven.[187] He marvelously
grants one the Pythian[188] art. He causes people to gather
before the exorcist as though he himself were the provisioner of punishments;
     they
are foreigners, since all murderers

---

187 *nocticorax* may refer to a number of different nocturnal birds.

188 Conjectural reading of *phitonicha*.

[305v]

suis tormentis trahuntur: fuit de ordine virtutum
pessimus est, et habet sub se .12. legiones.

Habet xxx. legiones.

Simias, ut Gumas magnus marchio apparet in similitudinem Leonis: equitat super ursum fortissimum, cauda eius
serpentina: flamma ex ore eius progreditur: In destra portat
duos magnos serpentes sibillos emittentes. Cognoscit vires
herbarum, et siderum: et loca planetarum, optime docet man-
siones eorum. Facit hominem transformare in aliam formam. Dat dignitates, et praelationes: Dat gratiam omnium   x
amicorum, et inimicorum. Habet in suo dominio 30. legiones:

Habet 30. legiones.

Volach magnus preses apparet in similitudinem pueri
habet alas ad modum angeli: equitat super draconem, duo habes
capita. Dat ad plenum responsa vera de occultis thexa-
uris, in quibus videtur seu apparent serpentes: si vult
omne genus serpentum tradit in manus exorciste:
et habet sub se .30. legiones:

Habet 21. legiones.

Gomeris ut Caẏm dux fortis, et potens apparet in si-   xx
militudinem pulcherime mulieris, duchali coronatus
corona, equitat super camellum. Dat ad verum plena responsa de presentibus, praeteritis, et futuris: et occultis caver-
nis, in quibus apparent serpentes est princeps, et custos
Dat optime amorem mulierum: et habet sub se .21. legiones:

are dragged off to the furthest places to be tortured. Of the order of Virtues
he was

the worst, and he has twelve legions under him.

Having 30 legions

Simias, or **Gumas**, a great marquis, appears in the likeness
of a lion; he rides upon a mighty bear, the tail of which
is serpentine; flames go forth from his mouth. In his right hand he carries
two great serpents uttering hisses. He knows the powers
of herbs and stars, and the locations of planets, excellently teaching
their houses. He causes a person to transform into another
shape. He gives dignities and prelacies. He gives the goodwill of all   x
friends as well as enemies. He has thirty legions in his dominion.

Having 30 legions

Volach, a great president, appears in the likeness of a boy
having wings in the manner of an angel; he rides upon a dragon with two
heads. He gives full, true answers concerning hidden treasure
troves, in which serpents are seen or observed; if one wishes,
every kind of serpent is delivered into the hand of the exorcist.
And he has thirty legions under him.

Having 21 legions

Gomeris, or **Caym**, a strong and powerful duke, appears in the likeness   xx
of a most beautiful woman, crowned like a
duke, riding upon a camel. She gives full, true answers
about things present, past, and future; and of hidden
caves, in which serpents appear, she is sovereign and guardian.
She excellently gives the love of women, and has twenty-one legions under her.

[306r]

Habet .20. legiones.

Cambea magnus comes Apparet in similitudinem fau-
ni: Cognoscit vires herbarum, et lapidum preciosorum: facit
etiam aves in terram descendere, et coram exorcista
volare. Et similiter ante se bellare, et velut do-
mesticare et ludere secundum suam naturarum. Habet 20.
legiones sub suo dominio:

Habet sub suo dominio 19. legiones.

Ẏudifliges ductor fortis, Apparet in similitudinem
corvi: et cum apparet in forma humana quando proce-   x
dit ante magistrum praeceptorem suum eo iubente: fa-
cit omnibus eum videntibus audire thubas, sẏmpho-
nias. Et transfert etiam omnia genera instrumentorum docet
canere: est optimus familiaris. Habet 19. legiones
sub suo dominio:

Habet .30. legiones.

Nuduch, ut Andrialfis Paelsis Apparet in similitudinem
pavonis, faciens quae magnos sonitus: et cum suscipit humanam formam Docet ad plenum Geometriam, et omnes
artes ad eam pertinentes. Facit hominem sapientem   xx
in artibus, et ipsum transmutari in speciebus avis: habet sub
se xxx.^ta legiones:

Habet .30. legiones.

Andras, ut vandras magnus marchio Apparet
in angelica forma, caput assimilatur nocticorati magni: equitat super lupum magnum, et fortissi-

[306r]

Having 20 legions

Cambea, a great count, appears in the likeness of a
faun. He knows the powers of herbs, and of precious stones.
He also causes birds to descend to the earth, and
fly before the exorcist, and likewise to fight before him, and, as though
domesticated, also to play according to their nature. He has twenty
legions under his dominion.

Having 19 legions under his dominion

Yudifliges, a strong duke,[189] appears in the likeness
of a crow; and appearing in a human form when, proceeding   x
before his master preceptor, he is ordered to, he causes
all who see him to hear
a symphony of trumpets. And he also carries every kind of instrument he
    teaches
one to play; he is a very good servant. He has nineteen legions
under his dominion.

Having 30 legions

Nuduch, or **Andrialfis Paelsis**, appears in the likeness
of a peacock, which makes a great noise; and assuming a human
form he teaches all of geometry, and all
of the arts pertaining thereto. He makes one discerning   xx
in the arts, and causes one to change into the likeness of a bird; he has
thirty legions under him.

Having 30 legions

Andras, or **Vandras**, a great marquis, appears
in an angelic form, his head like that of
a great night raven: riding upon a great and

---

189 *ductor*, rather than the conventional *dux*; lit. "leader", "commander".

[306v]

mum: gladium portat magnum, et accutissimum: ab eo
procedunt rixae, discordiae et eas bene scit seminare
videlicet inter duos fratres, Inter <ductum>, et <secuutum>: et habet
sub se 30. legiones:

Habet 30. legiones.

Saẏlmon, ut Zamon dux fortis, et preses, atque comes Apparet in similitudinem hominis: equitat super equum
pallidum, caput eius Leonis, in manu ferens aquilla,
loquitur rauca voce. Facit pacem inter multos
et discordes viros, sive feminas: et habet sub se .30. legiones: x

Habet 20. legiones.

Azo, ut oze magnus preses apparet in similitudinem
Leopardi: sed cum suscipit humanam formam. Reddit hominem sapientem in omnibus artibus liberalibus
Dat vera responsa de divinis, et occultis rebus: facit
hominem in aliam formam transmutari, et praecepto exorciste
facit hominem insanire: et putat se esse quod non est.
Et quia habet coronam in capite, et sceptrum in manu exis-
timat se esse regem: quod sceptrum tenet per spatium
unius hore, et quod exorciste patet, facit. Habet sub se   xx
xx.[ii] legiones:

Habet .26. legiones.

Bachimẏ, ut Albermi, ut Cabeẏm dux magnus et fortis Apparet cum tribus capitibus: primum assimilatur
Nason: secundum assimilatur homini habenti duo corpora

[306v]

mighty wolf, carrying a great and very sharp sword; from him
arise quarrels and discords, and he knows well how to sow these,
such as between two brothers, or between a leader and follower. And he has
thirty legions under him.

Having 30 legions

Sailmon, or **Zamon**, a strong duke, and president, and even
a count, appears in the likeness of a man riding upon a
pale horse, his head that of a lion, carrying an eagle in his hand,
speaking in a harsh voice. He makes peace among many
quarreling men or women, and he has thirty legions under him.   x

Having 20 legions

Azo, or **Oze**, a great president, appears in the likeness
of a Leopard, but assuming a human form he renders one
discerning in all the liberal arts.
He gives true answers about things divine and secret; he causes
one to transform into another shape, and, commanded by the exorcist,
makes a person become insane, and judge themself to be what they are not.
And because they have a crown on their head, and a scepter in hand, they
suppose they are a king; which scepter they hold for the space
of one hour, and which the exorcist provides. He has   xx
twenty legions under him.

Having 26 legions

Bachimy, or **Albermi**, or **Cabeïm**, a great and strong duke,
appears with three heads: the first like
a nose;[190] the second like that of a man having two bodies;

---

190 Conjectural reading of *Nason*.

[307r]

tercium muriligo: equitat super viperam portantem
in manibus vascham ardentem. Reddit hominem ingeniosum in omnibus artibus: et dat vera responsa. Et habet sub se 26. legiones.

Habet 20. legiones.

Arabas, ut Accabas, ut irabas magnus princeps
Apparet in similitudinem equi: sed cum suscipit formam
humanam virtute divina. Dat vera responsa de
praeteritis, presentis, et futuris: Dat dignitates et praelationes, et gratiam amicorum, et inimicorum. Habet sub se   x
xx.^{ti} Legiones:

Habet .30. legiones.

Balpala Dux magnus, et fortis Apparet in similitudinem leonis: habet alas ad instar Grifonis. Subtilis, et
mirabilis in Mathematicha, in Phisicha speculativa:
et in Chiromantia, et in omnibus artibus quae in mathe-
maticis libri inveniuntur. Habet sub se 30. legiones:

Habet .20. Legiones.

Lanima, ut <pruunas>[191] magnus comes apparet in ange-
lica speciem, sermonibus blandis aloquitur: et cognoscit   xx
vires herbarum, et habet sub se 20. legiones:

**De ordine Cherubẏn. Habet .40. legiones partim de ordine
virtutum, et**

Nunc autem de rege Paimon tractandum est, et est sci-   **partim de ordine**
endum quod iste paẏmon magnus: magis obedit vo-   **potestatum:**
luntatem Luciferum quorum alii reges Lucifer non est

---

191 *pruunā* in the ms.

[307r]

the third, a cat. He rides upon a viper, carrying
in his hand a blazing torch.[192] He renders one ingenious
in all the arts, and gives true
answers. And he has twenty-six legions under him.

Having 20 legions

Arabas, or **Accabas**, or **Irabas**, a great prince,
appears in the likeness of a horse, but assuming a
human form by divine virtue he gives true answers about
things past, present, and future; he gives dignities and
prelacies, and the goodwill of friends as well as enemies. He has   x
twenty legions under him.

Having 30 legions

Balpala, a great and strong duke, appears in the likeness
of a lion; he has wings like those of a griffon. He is precise, and
marvelous in mathematics, in speculative physics,
and in chiromancy; and in all the arts which
are found in the books of the mathematicians.[193] He has thirty legions under
  him.

Having 20 legions

Lanima, or **Pruunas**, a great count, appears in an angelic
semblance, conversing in an agreeable manner; and he knows   xx
the powers of herbs, and has twenty legions under him.

Of the order of Cherubim; he has 40 legions, partly of the order of Virtues, and
[194]But now King **Paimon** is to be dealt with, and it is to be   *partly of the order*
known that great Paimon himself is more obedient   *of Powers*
to the will of **Lucifer** than that of the other kings.

---

192 Reading *facem* for *vascham*.

193 A term which often implied astrologers as well.

194 Regarding the following entries for Paimon and Belial, cf. the corresponding treatment in
   Weyer, *Pseudomonarchia Daemonum*; it clearly shares a source with **MS Plut.** 89 sup. 38, though
   the latter bears significant variations which frequently alter the sense of the text.

[307v]

computandus ordo profunditas scientiae suae expandens vo-
luit Deo equari: et per superbiam eius proiectus est ad
exularem locum. Iste paẏmon cogitur virtute divina
et apparet multis: Cum autem coram exorcista venerit,
equitat super dromodarium lucidissima corona coronatus vultus huius fuscus: et antequam procedit exorciste cum tibiis, et cimbalis, et cum generibus ministro-
rum venient cum ingenti clamore, et rugitu. Alii
mitissimi sicut in arte salomonis id est in <exeuponti-
cha> optime declaratur. Etiam iste paẏmon lin-   x
gua sua, nec ab exorcista valeat intelligi: si exor-
cista sit intrepidus, quam ei distincte, et aperte loquetur
de omnibus interrogantis: Est enim memoratus dicit
de omnium scientiam ac philosophia, et de omnibus archanis, et occultis:
et scit disponere mundum, et qualiter sit de terra disposita: et quid sustinet eam: quid sit ipsa aqua, et quid
abẏssus: et quid ventus, et aquo loco exit: et si erunt
venti, et preceteris aliis. Loquitur de statu. Facit consecrationes tam de libris, quam de aliis rebus. Dat
optime dignitates; et omnes resistentes, facit humi-
liare, et voluntati exorciste satisfacere: et in   xx
super dat optimos familiares: et intellectum omnium
avium. Nota si exorcista dictus Paẏmonem ante
suam presentiam venire fecerit, caveat sibi ne
respiciat nisi contra Aquilonem qua ibi est habitatio

The order of Lucifer is not to be reckoned.

God willed the depth of their knowledge to be expanded, and for his pride he
    has been cast out to

a place of exile. Paimon himself is compelled by divine virtue,

and appears multiform, but when he comes before the exorcist,

he rides upon a camel, crowned with a crown most bright,

his face dark; and he appears before the

exorcist with pipes and cymbals, and with various sorts of

attendants approaching with enormous clamor and roaring. The others

are most mild, just as in the art of Solomon, that is in

exeuponticha,[195] it is excellently testified. Yet Paimon's   x

language shall not be able to be understood by the exorcist; if the

exorcist is fearless, then Paimon will speak to him as lucidly and fittingly
    as can be

concerning every inquiry. Indeed, it is recounted that he speaks

of all learning and philosophy, and of everything secret and hidden;

and he knows the disposition of the cosmos, and how the world

is arranged, and what holds it up; what is the very water, and what

the abyss; and what the wind, and from what place it departs; and if it will be

windy, and all the rest. He speaks of the state. He performs consecrations

of books, as well as of other things. He

excellently give dignities, and he makes all opponents   xx

humble themselves and satisfy the exorcist's will; and

moreover he gives very good familiars, and the understanding of all

birds. Note, if the exorcist

calls for Paimon to come before him, he shall beware

to look nowhere except toward the north, in which place

---

195 This word in the ms. remains uninterpretable, but cf. the equally obscure *Empto. Salomonis* in
    Weyer's entry for Paymon.

[308r]

sua: cum vero ad presentiam suam venerit sine timore
cum omni affabilitate eum suscipiat, et eum interroget:
et petat quod voluerit, et sine dubio optinebit:
Caveat igitur exorcista ne creatorem suum propter illa quae
promissa fuerunt ab ipso oblivioni tradat: sunt
quidam qui dicunt istum de ordine dominationum fuisse.
Sed ut mihi videtur de ordine Cherubẏn, et habet
40. legiones: partim de ordine virtutum, et partim
de ordine potestatum. Notandum est quod si memoratus
Paẏmon si solus venerit ut vocatus sunt procet quam   x
libanum seu sacrificium: ut si coactus sunt: semper cum
eo duo magni reges veniunt scilicet Belial, et Basaam, et reges alii magni atque potentes: 25. legiones semper cum eo in circuitum eius sunt: quorum
spiritus quod ex eis erunt non semper cum illo pergunt, nisi
virtute divina cogantur:

**Belial habet sub suo dominio 30. legiones partim de ordine Troni,
et partim de ordine**

Nunc de Belial rege non est scilendum, et primo   **angellorum: fuit de**
de suo dominio, et potestate, et eius sapientia: quod de   **ordine angellorum:**
ordine angellorum fuit, et inter eos fulgebat.   xx
Et ideo sunt quidam qui dicunt ipsum statim post
Luciferum fuisse creatus, et non affirmant quod
iste praeter fuit et deductor aliorum quae de ordine
ceciderunt, cecidit: et primus inter alios dignior
est, et sapientior, quid igitur si iste praecedebat

[308r]

is Paimon's habitation,[196] but then Paimon shall come before the exorcist
	without fear,
assuming every courtesy toward him, and the exorcist shall question him,
and beg what he wish, and without doubt obtain it.
The exorcist shall not beware, therefore, his creator on account of those who
were promised by him that he would deliver them into oblivion. There are
some who say this one was of the order of Dominions,
but as I see it, of the order of Cherubim; and he has
forty legions: partly of the order of Virtues, and partly
of the order of Powers. It is to be noted, should it be remembered, that
if Paimon should come alone as he is called, he shall demand as much			x
frankincense or sacrifice as if they all had been conjured. Always with
him come two great kings, namely **Belial** and
Basaam, and other kings great and powerful; twenty-five
legions are always with him in his train, which
spirits, belonging to the others, do not always proceed with him, unless
by divine virtue they are compelled.
> *Belial has 30 legions under his dominion, partly of the order of Thrones, and partly of*
> *the order*
Now it is not to be kept silent[197] concerning king **Belial**, and first of all
> *of Angels; he himself was of*
regarding his dominion, and power, and his wisdom; that he
> *the order of Angels*[198]
was of the order of Angels, and illustrious among them.						xx
And thus there are some who say that he was
created immediately after **Lucifer**, and do not maintain that
moreover he was also the leader of the others who
fell from that order when he fell; and he is first among all the others in
dignity, and wisest, for which reason if he surpassed

---

196 Evidently not his exclusive habitation, as he shares it with Egym and possibly others; see 309v.

197 Reading *silendum* for *scilendū* in the ms.

198 The text italicized here is partially written in the right-hand margin of the ms.; cf. the
	corresponding transcription.

[308v]

Michaelem, et alios bonos angelos caelestes qui de ordine
existunt quam vis ipse Belial ad sui ad terram proiecti
praecedebat omnes enim alios qui in caelo permanserunt, non
praecedebat igitur iste:
Belial virtute divina cum sufficit sacrificia, munera
et holocausta dat ẏmolantibus sibi vera responsa: sed
non ad plenam horam stat in veritate: nisi cogatur
virtute divina. Apparet in angelica forma Pil-
lech valde equitat super ignorum: blande loquitur
Dat dignitates, et praelationes. Dat gratiam amicorum.   x
Dat optimos familiares: habet in suo dominio
30. legiones, partim de ordine Troni, et partim
de ordine angellorum. Nota quod belial sibi sacrificantibus, semper mendax est: qui et humilis esse
voluerit cum spirituum vinculo ligatur cum quo sapien-
tissimus Salomon cum omnibus legionibus suis, ipsum
religavit: et religati sunt reges cum omnibus legionibus eorum. Bilech rex fuit unus, et primus
exeat post Cabelial. Deinde Asmodaẏ, et ceteri quae
quem credimus ipsos fuisse <emillmus>, et mille le-   xx
giones inter omnes. Hoc procul dubio Avi, Agron Solo-
mone dedici scilicet qua de re ipsos religavit mihi
non est dicendus: cedo eis quae propter arrogantiam Belial
Belech:
Sunt tamen quidam nigromantici pessimi qui affirmant

Michael and the other good celestial angels who
are of that order, by whose power Belial himself was cast to the earth,
who indeed surpassed all others who remained in Heaven,
Lucifer did not therefore surpass him.
Belial, by divine virtue, supplied with sacrifices, services,
and burnt offerings to him, gives true answers; but
he does not remain truthful for a whole hour unless compelled
by divine virtue. **Bilech**[199] appears in an angelic form,
riding vigorously upon who-knows-what,[200] speaking flatteringly.
He gives dignities and prelacies. He gives the goodwill of friends.   x
He gives very good familiars; he has
thirty legions in his dominion, partly of the order of Thrones, and partly
of the order of Angels. Note that Belial, having been
sacrificed to, continues to be deceitful, and he shall be
willing to be humble when, like the spirits, he is bound by a constraint like that
    with which
most wise Solomon
bound him with all his legions; and the kings remain bound with all
their legions. King Bilech was the first and only one
to depart after **Cabelial**. Then **Asmoday**, and the others who
trusted them were in the thousands,[201] and a thousand   xx
legions in all. This is far from the uncertainty regarding **Avi**,
called **Agron** by Solomon, namely as regards his binding of them, which
has not been spoken of to me; I yield to those who approach the
    presumptuousness of Belial,
or Bilech.
Yet there are some of the worst necromancers who assert that

---

199 Reading *Pilech* in the ms.; see infra. This name appears to be functioning here as an agnomen
    of Belial, rather than indicating another individual.

200 *ignorum* in the ms.

201 Reading *millibus* for *emillmus* in the ms.

[309r]

ipsum Salomonem eos religasse eo qua quandam die se-
ductus fuit ad instantiam cuius dat mulieris qua oran-
do inclinavit versus simulacra quidam nomine
praedicte Belial quod non credendum ẏmo fatuum est:
sed ut dictu est propter arogantiam omnes religati fuerunt
in magno, et proiecti fuerunt extra terram promis-
sionis in Babilonia in puteo valde magno sa-
pientissimus Salomon religavit: existimaverunt
<hitantes> in Babiloniam magnum thexaurum inve-
nire invenerunt concilium <unanimitus>[202], et asscen-   x
serunt ad puteum discoperientes confregerunt, et cum tri-
vio exiverunt: qui capiti in clusi fuerunt continuo
reversi sunt ad loca propria. Iste vero Belial intra-
vit quedam simulacra, et dabat responsa ẏrudan-
tibus eis et sacrificantibus ipsius: ut testatur Daniel
in sacris suis dictis babilolenses adoraverunt eum,
et sacrificabant ei:

De ordine Cerubin. Habet 1000. legiones
Egẏm rex magnus et fortis apparet in similitudinem
hominis: facies eius clara, flamma ex ore eius proce-   xx
dit: et equitat super draconem, et corona coronatus.
Habet bonos dentes. In dextra serpentes binos sẏ-
billos emittentes, venient cum ingenti strepitu
et clamore, et rugitu: et erunt ante ipsum omnia
genera instrumentorum, organa dulcissima. Docet

---

202 *unaminitus* in the ms.

Solomon himself, who bound them, one day
was seduced to the worship of one who gave him a woman, whose
pleading inclined him toward idols,[203] a certain one being
the aforementioned Belial by name, which is not to be believed; indeed it is
    foolish.
But as it is said, because of their arrogance all were bound
completely,[204] and were expelled from the promised land
into Babylonia,
bound in exceedingly great putrescence by the most wise Solomon.
Priests[205] in Babylonia thought to discover a great treasure,
having arrived at a unanimous council, and   x
agreed to break into an underground chamber and lay it open, and
bring it forth with ease: whereby those chiefs who had been imprisoned
were at once returned to their proper places. But Belial himself
entered into some idols, and was giving learned answers
to them, and receiving sacrifices,[206] as Daniel witnesses
in his sacred testament, the Babylonians adored him,
and made sacrifices to him.
    Of the order of Cherubim, having 1000 legions
Egym, a great and strong king, appears in the likeness
of a man, clear of countenance, flames   xx
coming from his mouth; and he rides upon a dragon, and is crowned with a
    crown.
He has good teeth. In his right hand two serpents
hiss; with extraordinary noise
and clamor and roaring all of these will come forth, and before him will be all
kinds of sweet-sounding musical instruments. He teaches

---

203 For one version of this story, and Solomon's binding of the demons in general, see Duling's
    edition of the Testament of Solomon.

204 Reading *in magno* as an adverb; alternatively, the scribe may have omitted a word which *magno*
    was meant to modify.

205 Reading *hierophantes* for *hitantes* in the ms.

206 Giorgio Anselmi discusses the binding of demons into oracular idols in his early fifteenth-
    century *Divinum opus de magia disciplina*, Biblioteca Medicea Laurenziana MS Plut. 44.35, 7r.

[309v]

ad plenum philosophiam, et artem canonicam, et artem No-
toriam: Loquitur de universis mundi praeteritis, presentibus, et futuris. Et docet de archanis, et occultis rebus: et de situ, et dispositione
mundi. Et qualis sit, terra. Et quid sit abýssus,
et ubi est. Et quid ventus, et ex quo. Et dat
optimos familiares, et dignitates: facit, et praelationes
confirmat. Et facit consecrationes tam de libris, quam de aliis rebus. Dat vera responsa de
omnibus interogatis: x
Notandum est quod si aliquis exorcista robustissimus Egým
ante suam praesentiam venire fecerit, caveat sibi ne
nisi contra septentrionem respiciat: quia ibi est
habitatio sua, et statim sibi appropinquabit: et ostendet
sibi sigillum, et anullum, et statim ipse in terram cadens
adorabit: et tunc exorcista faciet in terra, sicut
mox est: ut benigne, et aperte ab eo quod voluerit
statim dicet. Nota quidam dicunt quod Sathan est
qui ad septentrionem venit, et in septentrione ha-
bitet primo aliis regibus sed non est credendum: Nam   xx
Sathan apparet cum tribus capitibus ut dictum
est, et equitat super draconem magnum. Cogitur
etiam iste Egým virtute divina, et apparet:
multus libenter suscipit sacrificia, et holocausta
atque libamina et munera: decipit homines

[309v]

all of philosophy, and the canonical art,[207] and the notory

art.[208] He speaks of the whole cosmos,

past, present, and future. And he teaches of

secret and hidden things, and of the situation and disposition

of the heavens. And what that of the earth may be. And what the abyss is,

and where. And what the wind, and from where. And he gives

very good familiars, and dignities; he grants and

confirms prelacies. And he performs consecrations, of

books as well as of other things. He gives true answers concerning

all that you ask.   x

It is to be noted that if some most hardy exorcist

should make Egym come before him, he is to beware not

to look anywhere except toward the north, for there is

Egym's habitation, and at once he will approach him; and the exorcist

    shall hold forth

the sigil, and the ring,[209] and at once Egym, falling to the ground,

will revere him: and

by means of him, as quick and kindly and freely as can be, the exorcist shall

at once accomplish abroad that which he wills to declare. Note, some say that

    Sathan is

the one who came to the north, and in the north

dwells first among the other kings, but this is not to be believed: for   xx

Sathan appears with three heads, as

it is said, and rides upon a great dragon.

Furthermore, Egym himself is compelled by divine virtue, and makes

    himself seen;

he very eagerly accepts sacrifices, and burnt offerings,

and also libations and services — he deceives

---

207 An archaic name for the study of logic; see Rees, 1819.

208 The *ars notoria*, a medieval system of prayer, ritual, and meditation for attaining, usually, mundane knowledge; see Fanger, 1998.

209 Most probably a reference to the Seal of Solomon, traditionally engraved on a ring in the manner of that ascribed to King Solomon (see Duling, 1983: 962), though conceivably the text's distinction between ring and sigil may suggest the latter refers to a particular sign or signature of the spirit in question.

[310r]

omnes qui sibi sacrificant: semper cum tribus regibus apparet, quando holocausta suscipit. Sunt enim quidam qui
dicunt, et affirmant ipsum fuisse de ordine Che-
rubin: in suo dominio habet mille legiones de
regibus et principibus, secundam ordinem dicetur:

Habet 69. legiones.

Ras magnus preses, apparet in similitudinem cervi
cum autem suscipit humanam formam, loquitur gra-
ve: Beluas facit languescere, et claudicare.

Dat vera responsa: Dat gratiam amicorum: habet   x
sub suo dominio Lx9. legiones:

Torcha magnus marchio, et dux fortis apparet
in similitudinem Grifonis: cum autem suscipit formam
humanam loquitur rauca voce dupliciter: Et
potest per ipsum omnes volucres ligare, et omnia volatilia
quae sunt supra terra, et in aere: qui si exorcista
sapiens fuerit unam avem exere faciet, et ipsam consecrari faciet sibi talem virtutem dando quod omnes
aves liget sub voluntate exorciste: ita quod omnes
aves coadunet in illa parte, ubi est avis illa posita   xx
fuerit: et emittant dulciter cantus suos, et sint
mansuete, et humane voluntati obedientes in
omnibus. Nota quod exorcista potest cum ea omnes aves ca-
pere subiectarum quod sibi placuerit. Dat enim dignitates exorciste
et illas confirmat:

all the people who sacrifice to him. He always
appears with three kings, when he receives burnt offerings. There are indeed
    those who
say and affirm that he was of the order
of Cherubim; in his dominion he has a thousand legions of
kings and princes, called the second order.
    Having 69 legions

Ras, a great president, appears in the likeness of a deer,
but assuming a human form he speaks
gravely; he makes beasts weak and lame.
He gives true answers; he gives the goodwill of friends. He has   x
sixty-nine legions under his dominion.

Torcha, a great marquis and strong duke, appears
in the likeness of a griffon, but assuming
a human form he speaks duplicitously with a harsh voice. And
he is able by himself to bind all flying things, and all winged things
that are above the earth and in the air; wherefore if the exorcist
is wise, he will fashion a bird to hold forth, and
consecrate it, given so excellent a virtue that
the exorcist shall bind every bird under his will, such that
he shall gather all the birds in that place where the bird   xx
was deposited, and they shall utter their sweet song, and be
tame and obedient to the will of man in
all things.[210] Note that with this the exorcist can
capture all the birds so subjected that should please him. He indeed gives the
    exorcist dignities
and confirms these.

---

210 cf. the various magical images, or *telesmata*, attributed to Apollonius of Tyana (see Marathakis,
    2020).

[310v]

Habet .25. legiones.

Ara dux, et Marchio, Apparet in similitudinem draconis: cum vero suscipit formam humanam mirabiliter
cogit omne genus serpentum. Si preceptor fuerit sapiens poterit omne genus <serpentum>[211] constrigere si sibi placuerit: et faciat fieri unum serpentem de quocumque metallo, et faciat consecrari: ut nullus genus serpentum
audeat in illis partibus accedere: et istud stabit ad
bene placitum, sive in eternum. Et caveat ne fran-
gatur ẏmago, quae statim virtutem ad mitteret.   x
Dat responsa de praeteritis, praesentibus, et futuris:
et habet sub se 25. legiones:

Habet 20. legiones.

Acar magnus Comes, Apparet in similitudinem cichade: et cum suscipit humanam formam, loquitur rauca
voce: et est princeps muscharum, et locustarum: et
cum exorcista voluerit, poterit auxilio huius praesidis
ligare Cichadas, et alia similia. Fiat ergo ẏmago
exere ut alio metallo, et apraedicto praeside consecrari
facies, ut dictum est. Prestat etiam amorem inter virum   xx
et mulierem. Dat vera responsa de presentibus, praeteritis,
et futuris: et habet .20. legiones:

Habet 30. Legiones.

Paragalla magnus marchio et comes apparet in
similitudinem militis: eius caput assimilatur leoni,
et equus eius ut flamma ignis: et potestatem super aves

---

211 *sapientū* in the ms., but a marginal annotation there supplies the more probable reading.

Having 25 legions

Ara, a duke and marquis, appears in the likeness of a
dragon, but assuming a human form he marvelously
gathers together every kind of serpent. If the master is wise,
he will be able to bind every kind of serpent if it should
please him, and he shall arrange to have fashioned a serpent of whatsoever
metal, and make it consecrated so that no kind of serpent
shall dare approach that place; and so it will remain at
your pleasure, or otherwise forever. And beware that
the image is not broken, which would discharge the virtue at once.   x
He gives answers concerning things past, present, and future;
and he has twenty-five legions under him.

Having 20 legions

Acar, a great count, appears in the likeness of a
cicada,[212] and assuming a human form he speaks with a harsh
voice; and he is prince of flies and locusts, and
when the exorcist wishes, he will be able by the aid of this ruler
to bind cicadas and the like. Therefore an image is fashioned,
which you shall hold forth as any other talisman,[213] and preside over its
    consecration
as advised, as it has been said. He also bestows love between man   xx
and woman. He gives true answers concerning things present, past,
and future; and he has twenty legions.

Having 30 legions

Paragalla, a great marquis and count, appears in
the likeness of a soldier, his head like that of a lion,
and his horse like a flame of fire; and he has power over birds

---

212 Or "cricket"; *cichade* in the ms.

213 *metallo* in the ms.; the inferred reading is predicated on the cast-metal talismans typical of this
    art.

[311r]

et animalia: et faciat exorcista fieri militem de
ere in manu eius gerens gladium quod sit acutum
et praecipiat paragalle ut consacrer praedictus miles:
Habet potestatem vulnerandi, seu interficiendi cum gladio
ut cultello tantum modo perfigendo: postea ponatur
in domo regis inter multos discordes, ut inter
virum, et uxorem. Et habet sub se 30. legiones:

Habet 30. legiones.

Ponicarpo dux fortis, apparet in similitudinem hominis
pugnantis, portans arma. Fiat ergo ẏmago erea huius   x
arma acuta, et faciat a, praedicto consecrari: et per ipsa
poteris ligare pedites. Dat amorem mulierum, ac
vera responsa de interrogatis. Habet sub se .30. legiones:

Habet 15. legiones.

Lambes magnus rex, et preses apparet in similitudinem
mulierum: loquitur suave praestat amorem tam ho-
minum, quam mulierum: Si exorcista voluerit omnes homines ad amorem suum provocare faciat ẏmaginem auctam
en cum vicinus fronte scribatur amor amore vin-
citur, et praecipiat: ut consacretur dando sibi talem   xx
virtutem, ut omnes utriusque sexus homines <accendantur>[214]
in amorem exorciste ita quod nullus praesumat contra
eum in alium facere ad tuum praesignant. Et
habet sub se .15. Legiones:

---

214 *accedātur* in the ms.

and animals. And the exorcist shall arrange to have fashioned a soldier in the
    likeness of

the master, carrying in his hand a sharp sword,

and he shall instruct Paragalla to consecrate the aforesaid soldier:

it has the power to wound or kill by the sword,

or to merely pierce with the dagger. Then it may be placed

in the household of the king, among the multitude with whom you quarrel, or
    between

a man and wife. And he has thirty legions under him.

    Having 30 legions

Ponicarpo, a strong duke, appears in the likeness of a

fighting man, bearing arms. Therefore an image of this is made by

    the master,   x

having sharpened weapons; and having been made, consecrated as aforesaid.

    And by this

you will be able to bind infantry. He gives the love of women, and

true answers concerning your questions. He has thirty legions under him.

    Having 15 legions

Lambes, a great king and president, appears in the likeness

of a woman, speaking sweetly, bestowing the love

of men as much as that of women. If the exorcist should wish

to provoke all people to love him, he shall fashion an ample image

of the master, with "love by love

be conquered" written upon the brow, and order that it be consecrated to give

    him such   xx

virtue that all people of both sexes are inflamed

with love for the exorcist, such that no one would presume

to oppose one so preeminent as you. And

he has fifteen legions under him.

[311v]

De ordine principatus .43. legiones.

Triplex, sive complex magnus dux, et marchio, Apparet
in similitudinem angeli pulchri: et est humilis, et fidelis omnibus
mandatis exorciste, et est ideo triplex: quia per eum possunt
omnia tripliciter ligani, et ideo potentior est aliis. Ideo possunt ligari volucres, bestie, serpentes, Basilisci, et
dracones in puteis, et cisternis: et facit ad voluntatem exorciste, reges, magnates, principes, et mino-
res ad voluntatem: super tronum sedere coronam huius
auream quae consecretur a, praedicto praeside, ad tempus   x
tale, et ponatur in aula regis, ut in camera:
et habet sub sua potestate .43. legiones, et fuit de ordine principatus: Amen:
Quando, et quomodo invocationes debent fieri, ac prae-
parari, et in experimentis operari: Nota quod antequam aliquod
experimentum, ut aliquas res volueris per invocationem operari:
Abstineas te ad minus per decem dies a, venere, et
vestes mundas in duas tecum balnees, et sis tonsus
et ungues rasis, et confessus: et in tali statu po-
situs ac si mori deberes: et nota quod quatruplex   xx
est invocatio. Prima est ad amorem. Secunda
ad discordiam provocandam. Tercia autem est ad conse-
crationem alicuius rei, sicut anuli, ẏmaginis, de-
narii, ut libri. Quarta est pro furtis, et thaesauris

[311v]

Of the order of Principalities; 43 legions

Triplex, or **Complex**, a great duke and marquis, appears
in the likeness of a beautiful angel, and he is humble and loyal in all
the exorcist commands; and he is threefold in this way: for by him
everything can be triply bound, and therefore he is more powerful than the
 others. Thus
flying things, beasts, serpents, basilisks, and
dragons can be bound in pits and cisterns; and he conforms
kings, magnates, princes, and
subordinates to the will of the exorcist, as he wishes: seated upon a throne, his
 crown
of gold being consecrated as aforesaid, he shall preside for
quite some time, and be established in a king's court or chamber.   x
And he has forty-three legions under his power, and he was of the
order of Principalities. Amen.

**When and how invocations must be composed, and
prepared, and performed in experiments:** Note that before any
experiment, or anything you wish to perform by invocation:
Abstain for at least ten days from women,[215] and
dress yourself with clean garments; bathe, and be shaved
and have your nails cut, and be confessed; and being placed in such a state,
you must also maintain that manner. And note that
invocation is fourfold: First is for love. Second,   xx
to provoke discord. Third, however, is for the
consecration of some thing, like a ring, image,
coin, or book. Fourth is in case of thefts, and

---

215 Italian *venere.*

[312r]

inveniendis: unde sciendum est quod iste invocationes
fuerit per lunationes, et tempora, et qualitates ipsorum
signorum ut in multis experimentis invenitur. Unde
si vis facere experimentum ad amorem considera quod
luna sit crescens: et sol sit in calido, et humido
aere sicut quando sol est in geminis, ut libra, ut aquario: quae sunt signa calida, et
humida, aerea, masculina, et sanguis, et medu-
la sunt eiusdem complesionis, et quia amor pro-
venit ex calore, et humiditate. Considerandum   x
est ideo qui signum sit simile in tali experimento quo
quando sol est in Cancro, quod est signum frigidum, et hu-
midum: tunc est bonum fieri experimentum ad dolorem, quia dum homo est in maximo amore
puta in thauro: quia sibi opponitur cancere
sunt contrariarum qualitatum. Item considerandum est, quando sol est in aliquo signo callido, et sicco. Tunc est bonum facere invocationes spirituum
et congregationes infernalium:
Item considerandum est quando sol est in aliquo signo   xx
frigido, et sico, ut terreo dum tempus sit sere-
num. Est bona invocatio quattuor regum infernalium quattuor plagarum mundi:
Item considerandum est quo quando sol est in aliquo signo
calido, et humido, aereo. Tunc est bonum fieri

to find treasures: whence it is to be known that these invocations
shall be according to lunations, and times, and the qualities of
the signs themselves, as is discovered in many experiments. Whence
if you wish to perform an experiment for love, see that
the Moon is waxing, and the Sun in a warm and moist
aerial sign, as when the Sun is in Gemini, or
Libra, or Aquarius, which signs are warm and
humid, airy, masculine, and sanguine; and
marrow is of the same combination, and therefore love
arises from warmth and moisture.   x
And so it is likewise to be considered how the sign is disposed for an experiment
when the Sun is in Cancer, which is a cold and
moist sign: then it is good to perform an experiment for
sorrow, wherefore while a man is in the greatest of love
with a girl whose sign is Taurus, Cancer
opposes him by its contrary qualities. Likewise
consider when the Sun is in some warm and
dry sign: then it is good to perform invocations of spirits
and congregations of the infernal.[216]
And consider when the Sun is in some sign   xx
that is cool, and either dry or earthy, while the weather is
clear: it is good for the invocation of the four
infernal kings of the four quarters of the world.
And consider when the Sun is in some
warm and moist airy sign: then it is good to perform

---

216 The association of warm, dry signs with infernal spirits is corroborated by a text on astrologically-
    informed necromancy in MS Rawl. D 252, 29r-30v (Klaassen, 2013).

[312v]

experimentum virginum, et puellarum, et non in alio signo totius anni:
Item considerandum est quo quando sol est in aliquo signo
ferreo, ut humido, vel aquatico sicut est in
scorpione. Tunc est bonum facere experimentum
odii, discordie, destructionis, et non in alio signo
totius anni:
Item considerandum est quando Sol est in aliquo signo calido, sicco, et humido: et tunc potest homo constrin-
gere spiritus malignos ad communionem dum mulieres viduas   x
corruptas, ut maritatas, ut puta in Sagipta-
rio, et tunc est bonum exorcismos facere:
Item considerandum est quando Sol est in signo ferreo
ut sicco, atque terreo <immo>[217] totum illum mensem non
debes operari, nisi invocationes de Ascaroth: et
Ashec est causa, quia invocatur in locis ne-
morosis, qui locus est frigidus:
Item etiam quando Sol est in signo ferreo, ut humido, ut
aquario, ut est in piscibus: tunc fieri debet invocationes nemorum, et aquarum etcetera. Hunc   xx
sequitur de qualitate <sed>[218] et transmutatione
Solis, et lunae etc:

De transmutatione lune per 12 signa Zodiaci:

[219]Videndum est experimentatori postquam visum est de qualitate, et transmutatione Solis: nunc autem

---

217 $\mathcal{y}$ in the ms.

218 f in the ms.

219 The margin here bears an elaborate manicule, along with the annotation ☽.12.

an experiment for maidens and girls, and not in any other
sign of the whole year.
And consider when the Sun is in some
fixed sign, whether moist or watery, like it is in
Scorpio: then it is good to perform an experiment
of hatred, discord, destruction; and not in any other sign
of the whole year.
And consider when the Sun is in some
warm, dry and moist[220] sign: and then one can
bind malign spirits to consort with women, widows,   x
and harlots, whether married or girls, whose sign is
Sagittarius; and then it is good to perform exorcisms.
And consider when the Sun is in a fixed sign,
whether dry or earthy: certainly for that whole month
you must not operate, except for invocations of **Ascaroth** and
Ashec, because they are invoked in
wooded places, which places are cool.
And likewise when the Sun is in a fixed sign, whether moist or
watery, or it is in Pisces: then
invocations of groves and waters must be performed, etcetera. Here   xx
follows concerning the quality, but also the variability,
of the Sun and Moon, etcetera.
   On the variability of the Moon through the 12 signs of the Zodiac
It is for the experimenter to see afterward what there is to see of the
quality and variability of the Sun; now, however,

---

220 sic.

[313r]

de transmutatione, et qualitate Lune per 12. signa zodiaci. Non dum fuerit Luna in signo calido
et humido: vel calido, et sicco scilicet signo igneo, et duo-
bus diebus, ut quattuor, aut sex post primam coniunctionem
fiunt dies oppositionis est bonum experimentatori exor-
cismum operare. Nam luna a, prima ascensione
usque ad diminutionem, est calida, et humida humore
flematico ubi gratiosa. Si luna <secta>²²¹ tercii, ut quarti
tuum experimentum incipias, et accipias primam prime: et
primam coniunctionem, et non secundum essentiam: hoc est   x
secundum primam sextam, hoc est tercia dies post
veram coniunctionem secundum nos: sed secundum compu-
tationem Iudei aliter, non de Iunctione signorum
cum sole sicut dictum est de luna: quia eidem simili
fiunt exorcismi:
Debet ergo quilibet exorcistor dies et tempora septimane cognoscere, et nota quas invocationes omnium regum:
et hoc tam regum quam demonorum sub illis contentorum
in primo somno fieri debent nam ante, ut
post erit frustra laboratum: nam sicut patet   xx
cuilibet experimentatori volunt de facili venire
nec expedire: sed prolungant quantum possunt ante
exorcistatorem venire: et dies, et
horam quas elegerit exorcistor ad convocandum, et ne-

---

221 *f.ᵃ* in the ms.

on the variability and quality of the Moon through the twelve
signs of the Zodiac. Not while the Moon is in a warm
and moist sign, nor a warm and dry one, that is to say a fiery sign; and for
two days, or four, or six after the first conjunction
occurs; [but] the day of opposition is good for the experimenter
to perform an exorcism. For the Moon from first increase
until diminution is warm and moist, [but] of a
phlegmatic humor when it is agreeable. If the Moon is divided by a third or
    fourth,
begin your experiment, and first begin in the hour of Prime; and
the first conjunction, and not the following one. It is essential here that   x
after Prime, Sext is the next [hour in which one might operate], [and] the third
    day after
proper conjunction is the next for us; but
the Jews calculate the next [day] otherwise, not by the joining of the signs
with the Sun, as it is said, [but by] the Moon.[222] wherefore
they perform exorcisms accordingly.
Therefore any exorcist must
know the days and hours of the week, and take note of the invocations of all
    the kings;
and this is so as much of the kings as of the demons bound under them,
that in the first hour they must be drowsy, for either before or
after it will be in vain to labor: for as much as   xx
anyone else, experimenters are apt to wish to arrive [at their goal] easily
and without exertion, but [the demons] will delay as much as they can before
coming to the exorcist. And
the exorcist shall choose the day and hour for convoking, and

---

222 This passage appears to be a somewhat confused reference to the Hebrew lunisolar calendar;
    the text, possibly corrupt, seems to conflate the calculation of lunar months with the practice
    of reckoning each new day from sunset.

[313v]

gotium perficiendum ante tempus suum veniet, et non finiat:
et sic nisi tempus sufficiens habueris, Labor tuus vanus
erit: et sic forte tibi esset confusio, et destructio, quam
sic forsan spiritus essent commoti, et acederes securus
recedere: et alicui ipsorum causaliter obviabis, qui
propter commotionem faciet tibi tedium. Item nota quod
quilibet potest facere exorcismos suos in quacumque
hora, excepta hora matutinali: seu dum ma-
tutini dicunt in sectas dei eclesia, quia tunc
Deitas dei demones expellit: quia hore sunt sa-   x
cre, et sic non est bonum facere exorcismos. Item
nota quod ad dolorem, odium in quacumque hora noctis
non est bonum incipere exorcismus. Et quia lo-
cutum est de horis noctis expediamus nos primo
de horis noctis septimane, et secundo de horis dierum:
Unde dico quod prima hora noctis est quae recte in
crepusculo sunt bone invocationes principiorum
demoniorum: et recte in aurora dum tamen non can-
tetur in eclesia parochiali: unde si exorcistor
aliquem principem invocaverit, si a prima hora   xx
usque ad secundam non venerit nullo modo eum ulte-
rius invocet. Sed incipiat recte in aurora, dum
tamen parochialis eclesia a, cantu horarum.
Et nota quod principes venient aliquando soli, alii
cum magna congregatione ut in hoc libro de

for the business at hand to be completed before its time has come and gone;
and thus unless you have sufficient time, your work
will be in vain: and so it happens that confusion and destruction may
       befall you, as
perhaps the spirits shall be agitated, and you shall be forced to agree
to withdraw peacefully; and therefore some of them whom you will encounter
will cause you weariness by their commotion. Likewise note that
anyone can perform their exorcisms in whatsoever
hour, except the hour of Matins, or while
Matins is said in the precincts of God's church, for at that time
the divinity of God expels demons, wherefore the hour is   x
sacred, and thus is not good for performing exorcisms. Likewise
note that for sorrow and ill-will, in whatsoever hour of the night
it is not good to begin exorcisms. And since
the hours of the night have been spoken of, we shall expound first
upon the hours of the nights of the week, and then upon the hours of the days:
Whence I declare that the first hour of the night, which is properly in
twilight, is good for invocations of the principal
demons, and properly at dawn, so long as there is still no
singing in the parish church;[223] whence if the exorcist
shall invoke some principal, if from the first hour   xx
until the second he does not come, by no means shall one
invoke further. But one shall properly begin at dawn, so long as
the parish church has not yet sung the hours.
And note that the principals will sometimes come alone, other times
with a great congregation, just as

---

223 Regarding this injunction and the following, cf. the markedly different rules given in Weyer.

[314r]

officiis docetur: et quando veniunt soli magis obe-
diunt voluntati exorcistaris, quam quando veniunt
congregati, cui soli plus timent exorcistaris quam congregati:
Marchiones coguntur in prima, tertia, quarta, septima, et octava horis: Nam si in prima, tercia,
quarta, ut septima non veniunt, scias certissime
quod in octava veniunt. Et nota quod si marchiones
soli vocati fuerunt plus timendum est, quam si plures
essent: quam quando sunt omnes subduntur magistro, et
plus timent magistram, quam si soli essent: x
Duces non possunt constringi nisi septima, nona, et
xiii. horis: nam si prima vice non veniunt, venient in alia nisi in ecclesia parochiali etcetera.
Et nota quod tu debes habere illud signum an-
pectus tuum, ut in fronte: quia aliter
non timerent te, sed quando videbunt te, et signum incipient tremere: et habebis quicumque
volueris ab ipsis: cuius quidem signi patet forma suprascripta: — Finis
Explicit. Rome. 4. Ianuarii. 1494. die Satur-   xx
ni. horam meridiei pulsante: —

[314r]

it is taught in this book of offices; and when they come alone they are more
obedient to the will of the exorcist than when they come
gathered together, being more fearful of the exorcist singly than assembled.
Marquises are assembled in the first, third, fourth,
seventh, and eight hours; for if in the first, third,
fourth, or seventh they do not come, know most certainly
that in the eighth they will. And note that if marquises
have been called singly their fear is greater than if more
have been: as much as they do so when all of them are subjugated by the
        magister,
they fear the magister yet more if they are alone.   x
Dukes cannot be bound except in the seventh, ninth, and
thirteenth hours: thus if in the first instance they do not come,
they will come in another unless in the parish church [the hours are being
        sung].[224]
And note that you must have that sign
on your chest or brow, because otherwise
they shall not fear you; but when they see you with
the sign they will begin to tremble, and you will have whatsoever
you wish from them — the form of which sign is, in fact, plainly
written above:[225] — The end.
Thus it is unfolded, Rome, 4 January, 1494,   xx
the day of Saturn, striking the hour of noon: —

---

224 *etcetera* in the ms.

225 This may refer to an image elsewhere in MS Plut. 89 sup. 38, e.g. the "pentaculum Salomonis"
     on f. 294v or the "signum ✠" which one is explicitly warned *against* making on f. 297v, but could
     just as well allude to an illustration in whatever source the copyist excerpted the present text
     from.

BIBLIOGRAPHY

Primary Sources

Bayerische Staatsbibliothek, MS Clm 849

Biblioteca Medicea Laurenziana, MS Plut. 44.35
— MS Plut. 89 sup. 38
— MS Plut. 89 sup. 41

Picatrix. Ed. and trans. Dan Attrell & David Porreca. 2019. University Park: Pennsylvania State University Press.

The Grimoire of Arthur Gauntlet. Ed. David Rankine. 2011. Glastonbury: Avalonia.

The Magical Treatise of Solomon, or Hygromanteia. Ed. and trans. Ioannis Marathakis. 2011. Singapore: Golden Hoard Press.

Weyer, Johann. 1563. *Pseudomonarchia Daemonum*. Ed. Joseph H. Peterson, Esoteric Archives, http://www.esotericarchives.com/solomon/weyer.htm. Accessed 29 July 2020.

Secondary Sources

Main Collections, *Biblioteca Medicea Laurenziana Official Website*, https://www.bmlonline.it/en/la-biblioteca/fondi-principali/. Accessed 29 July 2020.

Pope Leo X, *Reformation 500*, https://reformation500.csl.edu/bio/pope-leo-x/. Accessed 29 July 2020.

Boudet, Jean-Patrice. 2003. Les *Who's Who* Démonologiques de la Renaissance et Leurs Ancêtres Médiévaux. *Médiévales* 44: 117-140.

Boudet, Jean-Patrice & Julien Véronèse. 2012. Si volueris per demones habere scientiam: L'*Experimentum Nigromantie* Attribué à Michel Scot. In *Rerum Gestarum Scriptor: Histoire et Historiographie au Moyen Âge: Mélanges Michel Sot*, pp. 691-702. Dir. Magali Coumert, Marie-Céline Isaïa, Klaus Krönert & Sumi Shimahara. Paris: PUPS, p. 691-702.

Brown, J. Wood. 1897. *An Enquiry into the Life and Legend of Michael Scot*. Edinburgh: David Douglas.

Brucker, Gene A. 1963. Sorcery in Early Renaissance Florence. *Studies in the Renaissance* 10: 7-24.

Clemens, Raymond & Timothy Graham. 2007. *Introduction to Manuscript Studies*. Ithaca: Cornell University Press.

Cox, Merlin. 2005. *Similar Stars And Strange Angels: Giorgio Anselmi's Astrological Magic*. Master's thesis, University of London.

Cummins, Alexander & Phil Legard. 2020. *An Excellent Booke of the Arte of Magicke*. London: Scarlet Imprint.

Davies, Owen & Francesca Matteoni. 2017. *Executing Magic in the Modern Era: Criminal Bodies and the Gallows in Popular Medicine*. Palgrave Macmillan.

Duling, D.C. 1983. Testament of Solomon. *The Old Testament Pseudepigrapha: Apocalyptic Literature and Testaments*. Ed. James H. Charlesworth. New York: Doubleday, p. 935-987.

Evans, James. 1998. *The History and Practice of Ancient Astronomy*. Oxford: Oxford University Press.

Fanger, Claire. 1998. Plundering the Egyptian Treasure: John the Monk's Book of Visions and Its Relation to the Ars Notoria of Solomon. In *Conjuring Spirits: Texts and Traditions of Medieval Ritual Magic*, pp. 216-249. University Park: Pennsylvania State University Press, p. 216-249.

Goldthwaite, Richard A. 1987. The Economy of Renaissance Italy: The Preconditions for Luxury Consumption. *I Tatti Studies in the Italian Renaissance* 2: 15-39.

Giralt, Sebastià. 2014. The Manuscript of a Medieval Necromancer: Magic in Occitan and Latin in MS. Vaticano, BAV, Barb. lat. 3589. *Revue d'Histoire des Textes*, new series, 9: 221-272.

Harms, Daniel. 2019. "Thou Art Keeper of Man and Woman's Bones" – *Rituals of Necromancy in Early Modern England*. Thanatos 8: 62-90.

Harris, Sylvia. 1959. The "Historia Trium Regum" and the Medieval Legend of the Magi in Germany. *Medium Ævum* 28: 23-30.

Kieckhefer, Richard. 1998. *Forbidden Rites: A Necromancer's Manual of the Fifteenth Century*. University Park: Pennsylvania State University Press.

Klaassen, Frank F. 1999. *Religion, Science, and the Transformations of Magic: Manuscripts of Magic 1300-1600*. PhD dissertation, University of Toronto.
— 2006. Magical Dream Provocation in the Later Middle Ages. *Esoterica* 8: 111-135.
— 2013. *The Transformations of Magic: Illicit Learned Magic in the Later Middle Ages and Renaissance*. University Park: Pennsylvania State University Press.

Marathakis, Ioannis. 2020. *The Book of Wisdom of Apollonius of Tyana*.

Rees, Abraham. 1819. *The Cyclopaedia; or Universal Dictionary of Arts, Sciences, and Literature*, vol. **XXI**. London.

Skemer, Don C. 2010. *Binding Words: Textual Amulets in the Middle Ages*. University Park: Pennsylvania State University Press.

Vaughan, Herbert M. 1908. *The Medici Popes: (Leo X and Clement VII)*. London: Methuen.

Williams, Steven J. 2003. *The Secret of Secrets: The Scholarly Career of a Pseudo-Aristotelian Text in the Latin Middle Ages*. Ann Arbor: University of Michigan Press.

INDEX

A

Acar 106, 107
Accabas. *See* Arabas
Afalïon 21, 23
Agron. *See* Avi
Albermi. *See* Bachimy
Alphas 84, 85
Andras 88, 89
Andrialfis Paelsis. *See* Nuduch
Anesa 40, 41, 42, 43
Antipalus Maleficiorum 4
Appolyn 65, 71, 73
Aquarius 113
Ara 106, 107
Arabas 92, 93
Ascaroth 46, 47, 50, 51, 54, 55, 80, 81, 83, 114, 115
Ascharoth 32, 33
Ashec 114, 115
Asmoday 99
Assasel. *See* Azazel
Avedie 76, 77
Avi 98, 99
Azazel 6
Azo 90, 91

B

Bachimy 91
Balpala 92, 93
Bamone. *See* Beduch
Basaam 97
Beduch 78, 79
Belfayt. *See* Berich
Belferich 46, 47, 50, 51
Belial 32, 33, 93, 96, 97, 98, 99, 100, 101
Belzebuth 72, 73
Berich 14, 15, 16, 17, 19, 64, 65, 71, 72, 73, 80, 81
Bilech 98, 99
Bille 78, 79
Boab 76, 77
Bonoreae 80, 81
Brulor 26, 27

Lightning Source UK Ltd.
Milton Keynes UK
UKHW050640300621
386397UK00006B/325